On Women and Judaism

ב״ה

To Ann,

with best wishes,

Blu Greenberg

Blu Greenberg ON WOMEN & JUDAISM

A View from Tradition

Philadelphia • *5742 / 1981*

THE JEWISH PUBLICATION SOCIETY OF AMERICA

Copyright © 1981 by The Jewish Publication Society of America
First paperback edition   All rights reserved
Third printing, 1983
Manufactured in the United States of America
Designed by Adrianne Onderdonk Dudden

ISBN 0-8276-0226-X

Library of Congress Cataloging in Publication Data
Greenberg, Blu, 1936–
    On women and Judaism.
    Includes bibliographical references.
    1. Women in Judaism—Addresses, essays, lectures. I. Title.
BM729.W6G73   296.3'878344   81-11779
ISBN 0-8276-0195-6   AACR2

Several of the essays in this book originally appeared, in slightly different form, in the following publications: *Hadassah Magazine; Tradition; Lilith; Sh'ma; Judaism;* and in *The Jewish Woman: New Perspectives,* ed. Elizabeth Koltun, and *A Coat of Many Colors: Jewish Subcommunities in the United States,* ed. Abraham Lavender.

To Yitz

Contents

Preface

AS the reader will note, the greater part of this book consists of essays that have appeared in a variety of journals, though I have taken the opportunity afforded by the present publication to make some revisions. Nevertheless, there is still some overlap here and there. I have tried to keep this to a minimum, but a certain repetition was necessary in order to flow logically from one idea to another within a given chapter.

There are also many issues that are not dealt with altogether. This effort was not intended to be an exhaustive analysis of women and Judaism, nor could any one person undertake the task. The Jewish tradition is a vast one. Even within the few areas that I treat, I have touched but the tip of the iceberg. This is the strength and wonder of the tradition, not its handicap. Thus, one must overcome the feeling of knowing nothing. One simply makes a beginning somewhere and then proceeds with a good deal of subjective feeling. I can only hope that those who know more, as well as those who know less, will be able to find something of merit in this work, either in the nature of a new perspective or in the encounter with previously unfamiliar sources.

There is, however, a unifying theme throughout the collection. It comes in the form of the questions running through my mind as I reflect on each particular issue. What position can we as committed Jews take toward feminism? What can we integrate, what must we reject? Where must we separate ourselves from mainstream feminism, and what are the pressure points in our tradition that, because we are women, we must locate? How and where ought the pressure to be applied so that tradition will neither discriminate nor close off certain parts to us? How can we become more responsible, fully equal members of a holy community? What claims do women have on tradition and Halakhah as the Jewish people move through the fourth millennium of their existence?

If I had to sum up my own position on the matter, it would run somewhat as follows: Judaism is my life. It always has been, it always will be. Feminism is a new ethical movement of special appeal to me because I am a woman. It is also of merit to humanity in general because of its ethical nature. Every person, particularly religious leaders, ought to search for ways to absorb and integrate its basic claim that women are equal.

I have tried to show that there are both precedent and process within the Jewish tradition for bringing women to a position of full equality. This process need not—indeed must not—be equated with a diminishing of the divine essence of Judaism and Halakhah. I am not unmindful of the tremendous sacrifice it took to bring me, as a traditional Jew, to this juncture in history. All those who preceded me labored hard to keep the chain intact. I do not want to break that chain. I do feel, however, that the link will be made stronger, rather than weaker, by a conjoining of feminist values with the structure of traditional Judaism.

I am pleased to make acknowledgment to the people who have had a share in this book. First, my parents, Rabbi Sam and Sylvia Genauer, gave me many blessings, especially that of growing up in a home rich with the love of tradition and Jewish learning. My children—Moshe, David, Deborah, J.J., and Goody—tolerated my erratic work habits and the expropriation of "their time"; they also made intelligent comments on many of the issues dealt with herein.

I give thanks to the many excellent teachers I have had over the years, particularly Nechama Leibowitz and Rabbi Meyer Feldblum, who taught me not only Torah but also how to probe the sources with questions. I am grateful to the many friends who, over the last decade, helped me to think differently about women. I also want to thank several people who contributed valuable assistance along the way: Rabbi Marc Angel, Roselyn Bell, Adina Feldstern, David S. Greenberg, Jonathan Javitch, Alvin Rosenfeld, Ruth Waxman, and Aviva Cantor Zuckoff. While their efforts have clearly made a difference in the quality of the individual chapters, they are in no way responsible for errors of fact, nor are they necessarily in agreement with the views expressed here. I am especially grateful to Maier Deshell, editor of The Jewish Publication Society of America, without whose gentle prodding, infinite patience, and deft editorial hand this book would not have seen the light of day.

Most of all, I want to acknowledge my debt to my husband, Irving Greenberg, from whom I have learned much in these past twenty-four years. He has not only taught me myriads of facts, but he has also influenced my thinking in a thousand areas; women and Judaism is but one. He read over my manuscript, in all its versions, and made countless corrections and suggestions, for all of which I thank him. My husband, of course, has spoken out himself on many of the issues discussed in this book. There are areas of agreement between us, as well as differences. For the reader who is curious about such matters, suffice it to say that there is much in this work that reflects his thinking. There is also a good deal that reflects my new ability not to back down in the face of his critique.

To the One who does not have to read my thoughts to know them, I am grateful for the blessings of life, good health, and love, which only God can grant or take away, and without which the body, the mind, the heart could not function.

B.G.
July 1981

On Women and Judaism

Feminism:
Is It Good for the Jews?

THERE is much to be learned from the women's movement that can enhance the quality of our lives as Jews. For feminists there is much to be gained from a serious regard of traditional Jewish values. Yet at this point the possibility of a positive relationship between the two seems improbable, if not impossible. Traditional Judaism has written off feminism as an extremist movement, a temporary cultural fad. Feminists have reviled rabbis as women-haters, male chauvinists, or, at best, men with ancient hang-ups. A religion and an ideology that under happier circumstances might have nurtured each other instead have become antagonists. Why?

The aims, achievements, and to some extent even the processes of feminism have been revolutionary. The fact that it has been a bloodless revolution leads some people to dismiss feminism as a petulant, middle-class women's hobby. Regardless, the women's movement has profoundly altered social attitudes toward women and the way women think about themselves. Increasingly, public philosophy and policy assume that women are full human beings with a capacity for achievement in all spheres in which men function. Women are no longer simply adjuncts of the men in their lives. Our secular, legal, social, and educational systems are under constant pressure to include women as equals; our religious institutions, however, lag far behind in the process of recognition.

Throughout the centuries, Judaism generated revolutionary ethical teachings. Why will it not now incorporate the lessons of feminism? Equality in various spheres long has been fundamental to Judaism; indeed, biblical teaching enjoins equality before law,

equal ownership of property, equality of all men.[1] Logically, therefore, should not feminist goals be embraced by Judaism today as a
means of achieving equality for men and women in the eyes of
God and the community?

Oddly enough, Jewish society—in which many pioneer feminists
were nurtured—was one of the last groups to grapple with the
challenges of feminism. True, Reform Judaism has taken many
steps in this direction, beginning with the call by the Breslau Conference in 1846 for full equality of men and women in all areas of
religion. This equalization remained largely formal, however, for
little of substance and leadership was given to women. Reform
Judaism made fewer religious demands upon both men and women,
and the changes it internalized tended to flow more from a simple
adoption of liberal or modern values than from Jewish considerations. Neither Reconstructionism, which pioneered in bat mitzvah
and in calling women to the Torah, nor Reform accepted women
for rabbinic training until the women's movement pushed them
across the line in the last decade. Even within these groups there is
still significant lay resistance. Basically, then, the response of the
Jewish community can be characterized as follows: the more traditional the Jewish community has been—or the more conserving its
nature (including elements within Reform)—the more likely it
tends to resist challenges from feminist ideology. This is as true of
women in the Jewish community as it is of men.

There are several explanations for this response. First, Jewish
women, on the whole, have been treated well by Jewish men, with
strong cultural values sanctioning such behavior. As a result, they
have been content to live within the traditional religious and social
roles that have been assigned to them. In practice these meshed
rather well: freedom from communal religious responsibilities, such
as synagogue prayers, enabled women better to fulfill the familial
role that Jewish society had ordained for them.

The second reason—and here we confront a factor more funda-
mentally resistant to change—is the halakhic model of Judaism.
Halakhah, the body of Jewish religious law, includes the religious
institutionalization of sexual and social status. In other words, what
was a sociological truth about women in all previous generations—
that they were the "second sex"—was codified in many minute

ways into Halakhah as religioethical concepts, binding upon future generations as well. What often is overlooked today is that, over the ages, Jewish tradition, by and large, has upgraded the status of women. It is true that in some centuries women were set firmly into disadvantageous positions. But for the most part, as the Jewish people moved through history, Jewish law granted increasing protections, safeguards, and even expansions of the rights of women. Thus, Halakhah influenced and responded to changes in society at large. One of the virtues of the halakhic system is that it has tried to maintain the balance of needs between community and individual, Jew and non-Jew, authority and freedom, religion and society. In this century, however, halakhic authorities have been concentrated overwhelmingly in the change-resistant sector of society.

The third reason for the traditional Jewish resistance to the feminist challenge—although this is not always openly articulated —derives from the widespread fear that feminist ideology poses an underlying threat to Jewish survival. Not lost on today's Jewish leadership is the fact that modernism has taken a great toll on the Jewish faithful—and so may feminism, the reasoning goes. Whether consciously or subconsciously, Jewish leadership is fearful of exposing traditional Jewish attitudes toward women to the claims of women's liberation movements. This fear is not completely invalid, nor is it restricted to the Orthodox sector. But feminism will not disappear by simply ignoring it or rejecting it as dangerous. Rather, the dangers should be identified and guarded against, within the context of a positive incorporation of the virtues of feminism into Jewish life.

Today, while secular society has opened up a new range of real roles and psychological expectations to women, the halakhic status and religious life of Jewish women remain circumscribed. It is like sitting in a stationary car alongside a moving one: the effect upon one passenger is a sense of moving backwards; upon the other, a sense of pulling away, of losing connection, of leaving behind. When confronted with harsh but often valid feminist criticism, religious resistance has taken the form of apologetics and defensiveness. Some Jewish women accept these prescriptions and rationalizations; others move closer toward the secular pole, abandoning not only observance but all traditional religious values as well. Since there is no currently sanctioned universe of discourse between feminism and Judaism regarding the religious status of women, the feminist movement often has attacked and rejected the basic structures and life values that Judaism has contributed to human society. This, of course, leads to further mutual estrangement.

What is sorely needed today is the creation of a dialectical tension between Jewish values and the mores of modern society in light of the far-reaching implications of women's liberation.

One crucial part of the dialectic is to measure the halakhic and religious status of Jewish women against the feminist notion of equality of women. There must be two-way communication and influence, not withdrawal and separation. An authentic Jewish women's movement thus must seek new approaches within Halakhah to absorb and express women's concerns and must seek to imbue women's concerns with Jewish values.

There are several areas in Jewish religious life where the goals of feminism may be applied creatively. This means interaction, not mere aping or assimilation. Though the truth is painful to those of us who live by Halakhah, honesty bids us acknowledge that Jewish women, particularly in the more traditional community, face inequality in the synagogue and participation in prayer, in halakhic education, in the religious courts, and in areas of communal leadership. These subjects will be discussed in separate essays more fully below, but here I will touch briefly upon some possible halakhic adaptations.

Family Law and the Religious Courts

Certain halakhic handicaps, which range from denying the dignity of women to causing them outright grief and injustice, warrant immediate attention. Jewish divorce law, for instance, requires that a husband write and deliver a get (a bill of divorce) to his wife in order for the marriage to be terminated. The effect is that the wife becomes dependent on the will of her husband in matters of divorce. This has led to the following problems: instances of extortion in the case of the recalcitrant husband; innocent suffering for the agunah, a woman whose husband is physically unable to authorize the get.

In this generation, sadly, divorce has become more prevalent; in contrast to previous generations, divorce now often is initiated by the wife. Many men, particularly those who were socialized to a male-oriented reality, are threatened doubly by this. Some base men even make use of the prescriptions of Halakhah to spite their wives, withholding the get even after the civil divorce has been granted, for they know that a Halakhah-abiding woman will not be free to start a new life until she has the Jewish writ of divorce in hand.

A further problem that grows out of this particular imbalance in Jewish family law is the divisiveness among contemporary Jewish communities. At one end of the spectrum are those who have dropped the requirement of a get altogether. A comprehensive solution, one that resolves the problem of recalcitrant husbands and will be acceptable to all Jewish denominations, is sorely needed. Halakhic leaders thus far have not treated with sufficient seriousness the proposed solutions that address these problems.

Jewish religious courts do not accept the testimony of women. A law that once protected women by preventing them from being subpoenaed into the public sector now must be reexamined in terms of equality of men and women. Although there are measures available that manage to circumvent this discriminatory law, none lends honor or dignity to the status of women. It is therefore urgent that contemporary legal and rabbinic scholars search within the Halakhah, as did their predecessors in times past, for solutions to end these iniquities.

Synagogue and Prayer

Although there is a range of opinion within the Jewish tradition with regard to women's liturgical obligations, none can dispute the fact that women have fewer prayer responsibilities than do men. Moreover, in communal prayer, which is the preferred form according to tradition, women have neither responsibilities nor rights.

Women are not counted as part of the minyan (prayer quorum of ten), nor are they called up to the Torah, nor are they permitted any service leadership role in the synagogue, such as rabbi, cantor, or Torah reader. These exclusions stem largely from the halakhic principle that women are exempt from affirmative commandments (mitzvot) that must be performed within a given time frame, such as morning, afternoon, and evening prayers.

The Talmud offers no clear-cut rationale for the principle of exemption. In a brilliant, succinct analysis, Saul Berman has shown that it is a rule with more exceptions than prescriptions: there are positive, time-bound commandments to which women are obligated, and there are positive commandments that have nothing to do with a particular time frame from which women are exempt.[2] Taken in its most charitable, well-intentioned light, the pattern seems to suggest a desire to relieve a woman of those obligations that may create conflict within her as a result of her domestic duties.

Given the new social awareness about women—their maturity, their ability to assume multiple responsibilities, and their increasing acceptance of roles that go beyond the home—the time now seems ripe for a serious reevaluation of the principle of exemption. A reinterpretation of Halakhah may lend itself to shrinking the period of exemption, that is, to obligate women to observe time-bound mitzvot, yet allow for exemptions during those years when there are overriding family demands. This exemption may operate until a woman's youngest child is seven, ten, or thirteen. The model to follow is the rabbinic principle: *ha-osek ba-mitzvah patur min ha-mitzvah* (one who is occupied in carrying out one mitzvah is excused from the performance of another mitzvah within the same time span). At the very least, this may resolve the problem of women being excluded from the *edah*, the holy congregation.

Sensitive halakhists must recognize that the general effect of exempting women from prayer conditions them to a negative or indifferent attitude toward prayer altogether. Women almost never pray at home; prayer thus becomes a function of intermittent synagogue attendance, hardly an incentive to serious prayer. Although the Law Committee of the Conservative Rabbinical Assembly did sanction the inclusion of women in the minyan, it did not take the necessary further step of equating women and men in prayer responsibilities. In Orthodox synagogues, where the *mehitzah* (the partition in synagogues separating men from women) tends to reinforce the inequality of the sexes rather than allow for separate but equal prayer, an intermediate and temporary step may be the formation of a women's minyan. Women thereby could develop the skills for leading prayer, understanding its organization and themes, and reading the Torah.

Prayer should not be a vicarious act but one of personal participation. At present, men generally perform for women even those liturgical roles that are binding on women, such as kiddush, the benediction recited over wine on the Sabbath and festivals, and megillah, the reading of the Book of Esther on Purim. The woman thus practices the commandments by proxy and often finds herself helpless if the male in her life is absent. Even if the proxy situation were to continue to give satisfaction to Jewish women—which is unlikely as their feminist consciousness changes—it operates only within the family context. Single women, divorcées, and widows cannot enjoy rituals by family proxy and therefore often are denied the spiritual nourishment such rituals offer. Moreover, such women generally are consigned to tangential roles in communities that organize themselves Jewishly around a synagogue.

Life-cycle ceremonies, such as brit and bar mitzvah, generally have had no equivalents for women, particularly in the traditional community. Similarly, rituals that celebrate biological events unique to women (such as childbirth and the onset of menstruation) are conspicuously absent in the tradition. To be sure, some women, often with the help and encouragement of men, are beginning to develop religious forms that bind up their unique psychic or physical conditions with Jewish tradition and the Jewish people.[3] In this regard, however, far more remains to be done.

Education

Halakhic education is the single most important area in reaching for the equalization of women in the Jewish community. In the Jewish religious-legal system, much leeway for personal judgment is given to *poskim* (halakhic decision-makers). Women decision-makers—one may call them *poskot*—are more likely than men to find sympathetic solutions for women's problems, for they share and experience them in the most intense, personal way. Considering how far Halakhah will have to grow to meet women's needs and overcome disabilities, it is essential that the community train women to become *poskot*. Until now, only men have studied and understood Halakhah, and they alone have made all the decisions; women have been kept ignorant of the processes of Jewish law. Today, women must apply themselves seriously to Jewish scholarship. There must be institutes of higher Jewish education, such as the *kolel* (communally supported talmudic institutes), where women can study uninterruptedly with some degree of financial security. Women must be trained to make legal decisions not only for women but for the entire Jewish community. It is to be hoped that the notion of women rabbis ultimately will be accepted in all branches of Judaism, for women can make a valuable contribution to the spiritual growth of the Jewish community. As currently structured, the community encourages a brain drain. Jewish women with fine minds are being wooed by secular society to make their contribution there, while the door to Jewish scholarship remains, in great part, closed.

Communal Life

The sociological and religious limitations imposed upon Jewish women have spilled over into areas of lay leadership in the Jewish community. In the past, there were strong obstacles to women assuming leadership roles. Increasingly, this resistance is breaking down, and greater numbers of Jewish women are beginning to play a more significant role in communal affairs. In many of the community's educational and philanthropic institutions, however, certainly in the lay functions in the synagogue, women are still barred from the top decision-making posts. It is as if the myth that only men are capable of making major decisions still operates in the Jewish community, even as it is being destroyed everywhere else. Jews often were blessed with great leaders; at other times, they have paid a steep price for short-sighted decisions made by inadequate persons who assumed power. As some contemporary communities sadly have learned, a highly successful businessman does not always have qualities that are transferable to communal leadership. Both men and women must begin to reformulate in their collective consciousness exactly what the requisites are: leadership abilities, a healthy measure of common sense, an abiding concern for the fate of the Jewish people, and a dedication equal to the tasks at hand. These qualities are not sex-specific. The question of discrimination apart, the community can ill afford to reject one-half of the potential pool from which to draw its capable leaders.

These are but a few of the ways in which feminist values can inform us as Jews. Necessary changes can be wrought in keeping with the tenets and spirit of Halakhah. This means using those halakhic categories that are clearly an integral part of the living dynamic of Jewish law. Halakhah need not be asked to conform to every passing fad, nor should *poskim* become fellow-travelers of every fashionable current; neither may the leadership hide behind slogans of immutability that are dishonest caricatures of Halakhah. Judaism throughout the centuries always has been open to other social philosophies as a means of upgrading and enhancing its own religious system. There is ample precedent for the integration into Jewish tradition of the best values of the society in which we live, especially where these illuminate or confirm central themes in Judaism—the dignity of man and woman as created in the image of God.

Marriage, Family, Children

We must go a step further. To be authentically Jewish means not only to take and learn from the broader universe but to serve as a corrective within the larger society. As Jews we need not buy the whole package of feminism. Rather, we must infuse our own ethic into a changing society and seek to check the excesses to which all revolutionary movements fall prey. The cosmic mission of the Jewish people throughout history—"a light unto the nations"—is no mere rhetorical flourish.

Thus, we must walk a very fine line, continually monitoring even those parts of the new that we have integrated into our lives to see whether they adequately meet our own tests. All of this implies an instant readiness to scrap whatever is antithetical to essential Jewish values, whatever bodes ill for Jewish survival. Feminism, for all its potential for upgrading the status of Jewish women, indeed has elements that are destructive from a Jewish perspective.

One of the by-products of the feminist striving for equality has been an attack on the family, as expressed in such familiar litanies as "the family was the locus of abuse" and "the family kept women down, back, behind, inside." The real impact upon women of such unrefined messages is to have them throw out the baby with the bath water, to abandon the whole enterprise without a backward glance.

The women's movement thus can be said to have made a not inconsiderable contribution to the crushing assault that has been mounted on the family by contemporary society. Signs of erosion are everywhere. The Jewish family, too, is beginning to crumble, as witness the unprecedented rise in the divorce rate among Jews and the alienation of husbands from wives and parents from children, with all that this portends for the future of family life. Young Jewish women openly discuss their suspicions about and objections to marriage, their intent to have no children. This is in striking contrast to previous generations, where marriage and children were a young woman's whole future and where (taking the matter to its extreme) there was almost a feeling of family dishonor if a young woman was not married off by the age of twenty-one.

Today we are wiser and acknowledge that not every woman can find happiness in marriage or in marriage alone. But given the prevailing pressures, we risk the danger of having the other option—a traditional marriage and family relationship—blocked altogether from consciousness and consideration.

All of this is particularly threatening to Judaism, for at the Jewish core is the family unit. The transmission of values—ethical, ritual, and philosophical—is effected largely through the family. The Jewish family has been the primary source of strength and support in coping with an often dangerous and hostile world. Today, particularly in America, this latter function of the Jewish family happily is underutilized, which should not mislead us into underestimating its other functions with respect to Jewish survival. In fact, new scientific research confirms what tradition has told us all along: the family is the most potent socializing and civilizing force available to us; it is also the single strongest determinant of religious commitment, values, and educational achievement.[4] Thus, the growing shift to school and synagogue for the transmittal of Jewish values seems a clear case of misguided judgment. Even those who see the havurah movement—the increasingly popular religious fellowship groups—as the educational wave of the future misjudge the reasons for its success. To my mind, the havurah is best understood as a unit that simulates a family. At its best, which can be very good, it is a supplement to or substitute for the family. It has evolved out of the search by many isolated young single people, as well as couples, for the proper framework to encompass their celebration of Judaism. Deprived as they are by the social forces of the traditional family unit, such individuals fill the void by creating its closest approximation, the nonbiological family.

Aside from the question of Jewish values, the issue of continuity is at stake. The earliest evidence on contemporary nontraditional human groupings indicates that these offer far less satisfaction, contentment, and stability than their proponents suggest. Furthermore, there seems to be a confusion of roles and responsibilities. Certainly, the family survived for so many thousands of years as an institution, with all its imperfections, because it was and remains the most ethical and viable of relationships.

For all of these reasons, then, feminists informed by Jewish values have another responsibility in addition to the call for equality. We must explore all possible avenues to strengthen the family and compensate for its limitations before casting it aside as an outmoded institution, one that no longer serves human needs.

First, we who call ourselves Jewish feminists must set the record straight: one need not engage in a total rewriting of history to effect change. It is true that the family was the context in which women functioned as the second sex throughout history. It is also true that other roles beyond those of wife-mother were limited severely. Today, in overwhelming part, neither of these conditions is a necessary concomitant of a woman's choice of role as wife-mother. Moreover, the family role was a source of security, honor, merit, and satisfaction for the majority of women throughout history, and that still holds true for many women today.

Therefore, the first step is not to denigrate the traditional roles women have occupied nor to hold in contempt those who choose them. Just as we reject the restrictive mold that confined women in the past, so for the next round of history we must not coerce all women into new restrictive roles that exclude wives and mothers. A case in point: the honorable phrase "working woman," as applied to vocations outside the home, undermines women's work in family roles. It belies the truth known to anyone who has done a measure of both: it is a more difficult task to raise young children, to keep a family and home going, than to do most other kinds of work. The new coercion, of course, is quite pervasive. How often has one found oneself engaged in casual conversation on any number of social occasions with a married woman, a mother of young children, who when asked what she does, mumbles, "Nothing." This woman probably has been on her feet all day, serving others, and giving love, but a flood of guilt washes over her just the same. She plays the game by the currently fashionable rules, succumbing to a truncated definition of creativity and productivity that doesn't come close to what a large part of life is all about—nurturing and being nurtured.

We must check the negative attitudes that abound with respect to raising children and see to it that such verbs as "mothering" are restored to our vocabularies as worthy options. More than that, since women are being bombarded with contrary messages, we must educate others to the pleasures and rewards of marriage and child-rearing. These are precious gifts and should not be relinquished so readily. Support of career women, single women, and women involved in political change need not imply denigration of the family. There is need to reintroduce into women's consciousness the perspective of a total life. Family, career, and advanced education must not be seen as options that exclude each other, for each can be pursued at different levels of intensity at different life stages. This kind of thinking may help women who respond naturally to the roles of wife-mother to feel less anxious in the face of contemporary pressure to choose one role exclusively or to be superwomen, pursuing everything simultaneously.

Another element in the safeguarding of the family is to teach society to open up more flexibly to women who have chosen the path of marriage and family. One subtle indication of prejudice by the feminist movement for career over family has been its ordering of priorities. The movement has mounted an attack for equal opportunity and equal pay for full-time careers, yet it has done very little about discrimination in salaries for part-time jobs, most of which are filled by mothers. Nor has the movement begun seriously to reconsider the adjustments necessary to help reintegrate a woman into a career after she completes her fifteen- or twenty-year stint at mothering. The woman who has been out of the work market for almost two decades continues to be penalized for this decision over the next thirty years of her life. This is an injustice to women, bad for society, and another negative factor in deciding whether to become a mother. There has been a conspiracy of indifference to this disability by both so-called male chauvinists and doctrinaire feminists. It is time for some serious efforts in this area. Society must be restructured to allow women a choice of roles, so that the whole matter is not simply reduced to a case of either/or. Bringing the husband back into a central role in the family, not just as provider and supporter but as child-rearer and involved husband, will push the whole process along that much faster; it will be a liberation of men, women, and children, too.

Happily, there has been some growth of awareness on these issues. Founders of the women's movement, such as Betty Friedan, have called for greater female-male cooperation in redressing the imbalance of society and for a critical affirmation of family and childbearing done in a spirit of true sharing. Unfortunately, the radical feminists have tended to dismiss or demean such views and this in turn has triggered and been used to rationalize the backlash against the Equal Rights Amendment and the women's movement.

Finally, there must be a corrective to some of the unrealistic conceptions regarding the newfound selfhood of women. This is as much an air-brushed version of reality as was the "little woman" image of the past. By and large, women no more can do it all themselves than men can. Loneliness and anomie are the real enemies of life, not commitment to human relationships.

Some women interpret women's liberation only in terms of their own personal needs, narrowly defined. This has led to a psychology of self-actualization that exclaims, "Let no one else's needs stand in my way." The result is a denial that there can be self-fulfillment in the process of giving to others. Any relationship of intimacy, if it is to last, requires the surrender of some of the self—disclosing, sharing, making compromises, yielding. This is as true for men as for women. Perhaps women of previous generations were overly generous in their yielding of self, but the proper rectification for this is not to be found in overcompensation. There is a point at which too great a sense of self is unhealthy, unrealistic, even destructive.

Building a marriage and a family, for all its satisfactions, must include a willingness to suffer some disabilities, to live with frustration. Not everything in life can be equal at every given moment. Good family situations are being exploded by unreal expectations and demands for immediate, personal gratification. The capacity to live with frustration has been dangerously weakened. Women, newly imbued with women's values, must not allow themselves now to deny the undeniable, and they must teach it to the men in their lives: for a marriage and a parent-child relationship to blossom, it takes time, energy, a measure of sacrifice, and generosity of spirit, all the opposites of instant gratification. To strive for perfection yet to live with less than perfection has been a classic Jewish response. Jews of today ought to share that message with the rest of society.

Contemporary Sexual Morality

Another issue that should be confronted by feminists and all others steeped in Jewish values is the new morality. Although this code of sexual license made its appearance well before women's liberation, the impact of feminism has been to extend the particular messages to the female population, thereby legitimating them for all. Formerly a man's prerogative and oppressive to women, extramarital affairs now have become a symbol of equality for women, undermining family stability and contributing to the soaring number of broken families. Because most Jews are concentrated in urban, higher-income, better-educated sectors, they are exposed to these new values—in contrast to previous generations, when Jews lived by an internal moral code. Although some of the bases of faithfulness and low divorce rates of previous generations were negative and coercive, the shift is a grim warning of the destructive potential in many well-intentioned feminist clichés, particularly that of sexual freedom.

Although Judaism traditionally has nurtured healthy sexual outlets within marriage and even recognized them before marriage, it put strict curbs on extramarital sexuality. In fact, two out of the ten commandments prohibit such liaisons. One need not identify with the male privilege or the double standard suggested in these laws to agree with the main goal of the prohibitions involved. The desire to engage in extramarital sex is not abnormal. The Torah spoke to real people with real passions and sought to lift these to a higher level. The difference, however, between the past and the present is that formerly these passions had to be contained within the realm of one's fantasy life, whereas the dominant ethic now pushes for their untrammeled expression.

As Jews, we must say that not everything one wants one may have, nor is it invariably good and healthy to let it all hang out. The whole structure of mitzvot has taught us that one is really free only within an ethical and moral structure. Given human limitations, ethics within an interpersonal relationship necessarily involves restraint or frustration. Judaism never outlawed divorce. It permitted divorce as a necessary, if regrettable, means to end an unsatisfactory relationship. But the parameters of the marital relationship, while it was being lived, were at least fidelity, holiness, and mutual respect. Feminists who claim that women now should have full sexual freedom define freedom as allowing the ex-slave the same right to abuse that previously only the master had. Jewish feminists should rather challenge and censure these values in male society. We should press for equal morality, not equal amorality.

Another aspect of the dialectical relationship between Judaism and feminism involves separating out messages that are good for society in general yet harmful to the Jewish people. Thus, in the era of "the vanishing American Jew," Zero Population Growth is no answer for us. To survive with a margin of safety, Jews need a population explosion, not ZPG. Of course, no one should be coerced into having children; giving birth only for the sake of Jewish survival probably will result in an unhealthy family nexus. As Jews living in the post-Holocaust age, we must be acutely aware that the holiness and faith in creating and enhancing life add a profound dimension of depth to the joy of child-rearing.

The Holocaust informs our attitudes toward abortion as well. As survivors of an era in which six million Jews were killed, one-fourth of them children, we have to consider both sides of the abortion issue. From a Jewish perspective, we must talk about the preciousness of life, not just about the right to life. A woman's right to consider the quality of life that she and her child will have should go hand in hand with education on the sanctity of life and on the risk of devaluating life in unthinking or easy medical solutions.

The halakhic outlook opposes abortion on demand. As Jews, we must demonstrate that abortion need not eliminate reverence for life nor joy in creating life. An orientation of this nature will allow new halakhic attitudes toward abortion. It also will help curb the facile, nonchalant attitudes toward abortion as well as the abuses that can grow out of abortion reform. The protection of the quality of life is the ethical basis of abortion, but this may be offset or destroyed by a loss of reverence for life. Abortion never must be allowed to become simply a preferred method of birth control. Halakhic guidelines that accommodate women's needs yet communicate this traditional reverence for life are called for.

If one is not locked into the narrowly focused battle surrounding the issue of abortion, many other possibilities emerge, such as the establishment by the Jewish community of adoptive agencies for pregnant Jewish women who cannot or do not want to keep their own babies. Carrying the baby to birth and giving it up for adoption should be an available option. The current universal dominance of the pro-abortion values among Jews has all but destroyed the availability of Jewish babies for adoption. This causes real problems for couples who wish to adopt.

The feminist movement has brought another unfortunate message of modern society—its materialistic orientation. Men's and women's worth are determined by what and how much they produce, what kind of jobs they hold, their titles, their earnings, and not by their values and characters. This has led to dehumanization, worship of success, and rejection of failures, including the poor. This attitude spills over into a critique of volunteerism. In part a reaction to the exclusion of women from high-paying jobs, women's voluntary and philanthropic efforts have been scorned. Such slogans as "Self-esteem comes from a salaried job" or "If it isn't paid for it isn't taken seriously" are no longer whispered. These ideas lead some women to abdicate responsibilities that used to be shared by all. Jewish charitable organizations, the mainstay of the Jewish community, are in decline because the ranks of committed workers now march to a different beat.

Jewish feminists must affirm the basic Jewish principle that the human being is valuable in his or her very being. We must articulate the value in serving, in giving of ourselves to others, in acts of lovingkindness that can be performed in volunteer work, in professional life, in being a good family member and friend. Not everyone can afford to work without pay, but this certainly should remain a respected option. Those who find satisfaction in giving to others should be praised, not scorned. The traditional role of enabling is a valid one as long as it is not limited to women, nor women limited to it. Every member of the community should be educated to his or her responsibility for the community.

We must attempt to infuse these values into the society we seek to create, rather than simply imitate the errors of the male society we slowly are entering. The truly revolutionary—and more difficult—task is to change the very frame of societal values. To rise above the production-value system, to reorient society, is to liberate men *and* women for a more human living.

We must check the excesses of those feminists who are against men, almost antihuman in their hostility. Jewish women do not need to hate men in order to energize themselves, nor should Jewish men be seen simply as crude oppressors of women throughout history. We do not require such cartoons to justify ourselves. For most of our history, Jewish men and women suffered together from external persecution and hostility; it was their mutual solidarity that carried them through. Instead of placing ourselves at opposite poles, we must try to liberate men so that, together with women, they will strive for a sense of dignity and human worth.

Finally, we must reject the notion that equality means androgyny. From the perspective of Judaism there can be separate, clear-cut roles in which men and women may function as equals without losing separate identities. Male and female are admittedly difficult concepts to define, but we must be aware in each instance whether we are dealing with the dignity of equality, which is an essential value in Judaism, or the identity of male and female, which is not. Jewish women who have identified with feminist goals have an added measure of responsibility in all of these issues, for they are in a better position to influence and be heard out by both sides.

It is no mean task to walk the fine line between old and new, status quo and avant-garde, tradition and change, God's commandments and the emerging needs of societies and individuals. But Judaism has survived considerable odds and has managed to contribute greatly to world civilization precisely because in each era it managed to walk that fine line. To keep the balance between these opposing forces is probably more difficult now—the forces are stronger and at a higher level of tension in our time, and society is more open. But our faith in Judaism and the Jewish people gives us the strength to demand and expect the same achievement in our time. It is a task worthy of the effort.

NOTES

1. Emanuel Rackman, "Equality in Judaism," in *Equality*, ed. J. Roland Pennock and John W. Chapman (New York: Lieber-Atherton, 1967).

2. Saul Berman, "The Status of Women in Halakhic Judaism," *Tradition* 14 (Winter 1973): 5–28.

3. See, for example, Arlene Agus, "This Month Is for You: Observing Rosh Hodesh as a Woman's Holiday," in *The Jewish Woman: New Perspectives*, ed. Elizabeth Koltun (New York: Schocken Books, 1976), pp. 84–93; *A Guide toward Celebrating the Birth of a Daughter* (New York: Jewish Women's Resource Center, 1980).

4. Geoffrey Bock, "The Social Context of Jewish Education: A Literature Review" (paper delivered at the Colloquium on Jewish Education and Jewish Identity of the American Jewish Committee, New York, April 1974). See also Harold S. Himmelfarb, "The Non-Linear Impact of Schooling: Comparing Different Types and Amounts of Jewish Education," *Sociology of Education* 50 (April 1977): 114–32.

Can a Mild-Mannered Yeshiva Girl Find Happiness among the Feminists?

ON occasion I have been asked: How can one so rooted in Jewish tradition, so at home with halakhic prescriptions and proscriptions, have such strong feminist leanings? Are the two not mutually exclusive, anomalous, contradictory? To the extent that one's worldview is shaped by small incidents, special encounters, and chance events, as much as it is by environment, endowment, and formal education, I would like to share with the reader some of those points along the route of a transition woman.

I was born into a strongly traditional family. With all the structure this entails, it was quite natural to be socialized early into the proper roles. I knew my place and I liked it—the warmth, the rituals, the solid, tight parameters. I never gave a thought as to what responsibilities I did or didn't have as a female growing up in the Orthodox Jewish community. It was just the way things were—the most natural order in the world.

My friends and I shared the same world of expectation. I remember the year of the bar mitzvahs of our eighth-grade male friends. We girls sat up in the women's section of the synagogue and took great pride in "our boys." If we thought about ourselves at all, it was along the lines of "thank God we are females and don't have to go through this public ordeal." Quite remarkably, there never was any envy of what the boys were doing, never a thought of "why not us?" Perhaps it was because we knew that our big moment would come: as proper young ladies growing up in the modern Orthodox community in the 1950s, *our* puberty rite was the Sweet Sixteen.

My short-lived encounter with daily prayer ended when I was fourteen. I had graduated from a local yeshiva in Far Rockaway, New York, and had begun commuting to a girls' yeshiva high school in Brooklyn. This meant getting up an hour earlier to catch the 7:18 Long Island train, so prayer was the first thing to go. I had it down to a science: if I laid out my clothes in exactly the right order the night before, I could set the alarm for 6:52, get up, wash, dress, eat the hot breakfast without which, my mother insisted, a person could not face the world each day, and still have time to walk briskly to the train. I would reserve a four-seater in the same car each day. Just as the train started to pull out, my friends who were attending the boys' yeshiva would come dashing down the platform and fling themselves onto the slowly moving train. I knew that they had been up since six o'clock to allow enough time for *shaharit*, the mandatory morning prayers. There they were, a little bleary-eyed, already spent at 7:18, with just a package of Sen-Sen for breakfast. Those were wonderful, funny trips. Though I laughed with the boys each morning, I certainly didn't envy their more rigorous regimen.

I also relished the tale told about my cousin Tzvi, then thirteen. He was on his way from Seattle to the Telshe Yeshiva in Cleveland. It was a night flight, and because of a delay and the change of time zones, the plane was still in the air as it neared time for the morning devotions. A no-nonsense thirteen year old when it came to religious obligation, Tzvi went to the back of the plane, strapped on his tefillin, and began to pray. In the 1950s, it took a lot of guts to be so conspicuous; many Americans, especially in the West, genuinely believed that Jews had horns. The Northwest Airlines stewardess, however, was not one of them. She gently put her arm around Tzvi and said, "What's the matter, sonny, don't you think you're going to make it?" Aside from the humor, I was very proud of my cousin, one year my junior, but somehow I never related his experience in any way to my own religious life.

In the fifties, the modern Orthodox community was just beginning to make its mark. Orthodoxy had suffered a terrible falloff in the aftermath of the great waves of immigration. There were several prominent rabbis in New York City—Leo Jung, Joseph Look-stein, Emanuel Rackman—who had initiated the process of re-establishing Orthodoxy as a respected Jewish option in modern America, but the process was still incomplete in the fifties. It took the turbulent sixties, with all that decade's variety of experimentation in self-assertion, before the rest of the country could accept ethnicity. And Jews were no different. For many Jews, it took the Six-Day War to invest them with enough self-pride to overcome a stifling self-consciousness.

Meanwhile, in the fifties, Orthodox Jews lived their lives with great fidelity to the Halakhah, even as they tried to "pass" in the larger society. After all, why bring special attention to a particularist way of life? "Be a Jew at home, a man in the streets" was the unspoken social principle. And how did this fine-tuning manifest itself? In one's dress, one's speech, one's name.

The evolution of the *kipah* is a case in point. In the fifties, this headcovering, incumbent upon every observant Jewish male, was still called by its Yiddish name, *yarmulke*—*kipah* is the Hebrew term—and it certainly wasn't what it is today. In place of those small, neat, attractive, finely crocheted circles you see everywhere nowadays, the 1950s offered only black rayon or silk, measuring a full handspan.

By choice and expectation, my social circle was confined to the yeshiva crowd. Although I don't recall ever discussing with a date how he felt about wearing a *kipah*, I could always observe the different ways of handling the matter in a public situation. One never saw a *kipah* bobbing down Fifth Avenue in the fifties. A hat or a cap was a bit more conspicuous in summer than in winter, but it wasn't all that outlandish. The big test, however, came when the young men entered a public place—a theater, a movie house, a library. Unless it was a restaurant, most of the young Orthodox men of my acquaintance, even the rabbinical students, would go bareheaded for the short duration (something their sons would be horrified at today). In addition, there were all sorts of permutations and combinations—putting on one's *kipah* before saying a blessing over an ice cream soda and then removing it before eating, or waiting until the lights in the theater dimmed before slipping it on. It wasn't that these things were done stealthily or with guilt. It was all a bit of harmless maneuvering to enable a young man and his date to feel at home in a wider range of social, public settings.

How did I relate to all this? With a sense of relief, for I didn't have to cope with the encumbrance of a *kipah* on top of the normal teen load of social self-consciousness. I can recall, in the early courtship with the man who was to become my husband, an occasional sensation of discomfort at the fact that he never removed his *kipah* in public places. Not to my credit, I even remember one evening at the opera, of which I didn't hear a word, while I sat thinking the whole time, "Why can't he be more sensible, less conspicuous?"

This is not meant to be a disquisition on the art of *kipah*-wearing in the fifties. Rather, it is to point out that for a young woman growing up at that time the lines were drawn sharply, and I was glad to be off the hook as far as certain religious responsibilities were concerned. It never occurred to me that these were overt expressions of a religious stamina, a formal statement of what a young man stood for. And although there were no guarantees that this was for life—many a young man broke under the burdens of *kipah* and daily prayer—it was still a more demanding path than that charted for a young woman. The ever-so-subtle side message was that male Jews who passed the tests were a superior breed.

I had a fine Jewish education, the best a girl could have. My father always was more interested in my Hebrew studies than in my secular ones, and he studied with my sisters and me regularly. My mother, the more practical one, also encouraged my Hebrew studies. Having lived through the Depression, she believed that a Hebrew-teacher's license was like money in the bank—the best insurance a girl could buy. Why a Hebrew teacher? That was just about the highest career expectation for a Jewish educated female in the fifties. We were an achievement-oriented family, so along with our secular degrees, my sisters and I and most of our friends added another notch to our dowry belts, a Hebrew-teacher's license.

The fact that teaching Hebrew was a low-paying career didn't matter much. In the fifties, a young Jewish woman really didn't have to worry about earning a living. It was more a matter of waiting for Mr. Right to come along and take over where parental support left off. In her inner soul, perhaps, a young woman's anxieties were greater: she had to wait, somewhat passively, for a man to create a future for her, whereas a young man had a sense of holding the future in his hands. On the surface, however, I think it was easier to be a woman. The loads were neatly packaged, and the one marked "female" was lighter.

After my marriage in the late 1950s, my feelings of contentment and fulfillment were enhanced rather than diminished. The ways of a traditional Jewish woman suited me just fine. All those platitudes about building a faithful Jewish home were not nearly as pleasant as the real thing itself. Moreover, none of those obligations ruled out graduate studies and plans for a career. It was a time of peaceful coexistence between the traditional roles and the initial stirrings of self-actualization for women. I considered myself very lucky to have a husband to care for me and I for him—a man, moreover, who encouraged me to expand my own horizons.

The religious role of a married woman was also perfect in my eyes. I found the clear division of labor, and its nonnegotiable quality, most satisfying. It never crossed my mind that experiencing certain mitzvot vicariously was anything less than the real thing. Quite the reverse. When my husband had to be away on the Sabbath, the act of my reciting the blessings over the wine and the bread for our small children only served to heighten my sense of loneliness for him.

The real thing, then, was for him to perform his mitzvot and for me to attend to mine. I wasn't looking for anything more than I had, certainly not in the way of religious obligations or rights. On those bitter cold Sabbath mornings I was absolutely delighted to linger an hour longer in a nice warm bed and play with the kids rather than to have to brave the elements. I could choose to go to the synagogue when I wanted or pray at home when I wanted; for my husband there was no choice.

The *mehitzah* separating men from women in the synagogue served to symbolize the dividing line. Although there were certain things about sitting behind the *mehitzah* that I didn't exactly appreciate, none seemed an attack on my womanhood. Not only did I not perceive the *mehitzah* to be a denigration of women in the synagogue, but I couldn't understand why some Jews felt that way.

At some level, to me the *mehitzah* symbolized the ancient, natural, immutable order of male and female. One didn't question such things.

All of this is not to say that I lived a perfectly docile existence within the boundaries of this natural order. There were certain incidents that made me chafe at the outer limits, but these were isolated, sporadic, and unconnected. I did not see them as part of any meaningful pattern.

During my junior year in college, I studied in Israel for several months at a Hebrew teachers' institute. Nechama Leibowitz was my teacher for Bible. She was the most brilliant, exciting teacher I ever had, and she became an extraordinary model for me. As the time neared to return home, I decided that I wanted to take a year off from Brooklyn College where I had been enrolled and just study intensively with Nechama. She was then teaching at fifteen different places, from army camps to kibbutz seminars to study groups for middle-aged Jerusalem ladies. My intention was to make Jerusalem my home base, follow Nechama to all the places she taught, and learn from her day and night. As an eighteen year old with a singular lack of ambition, it was about the only unusual thing I cared to do. "Come home and finish college," said my parents. "You're crazy," said most of my friends. In the back of my mind, I guess I somehow knew, back in the fifties, that it wasn't the sort of thing a nice Orthodox Jewish girl would do. Not being assertive or terribly independent, I came home to work on Nechama's famous *gilyonot* (Bible questionnaires) and move quickly into the next slot. But even as I did, I quietly knew that had I been a young man wanting to stay on and study intensively with a special Israeli rebbe, every encouragement would have been forthcoming.

Another incident that gave pause for thought was the *oyfruf* of my cousin Allan. (This is the ceremony of calling up a bridegroom to read from the Torah in the synagogue on the Sabbath preceding the wedding.) The *oyfruf* was to be held at a synagogue a mile from where we lived at the time. I was looking forward to the occasion because many of my relatives from Seattle, whom I hadn't seen for a long time, would be there. I had arranged with the baby-sitter to come at 9:30; my husband had left an hour earlier to catch the beginning of the services. The appointed hour passed, then 10:00, 10:30, and still no baby-sitter. At that time there was no eruv (a circumferential boundary that transforms the legal nature of property) in Manhattan that would have permitted me to push a carriage on the Sabbath; there was simply no way I could walk with an infant and a toddler to the synagogue, a mile away. I sat there for an hour, all dressed up, wearing my hat, muttering darkly at the world, while my two young sons played at my feet. Though I couldn't put my frustration into any sort of framework, I had a vague feeling that above my own failure to make any contingency arrangements, there were some situations in which the demarcations brought me up short. If synagogue weren't a man's thing, I mentally pouted, then somehow it would have been I and not my husband at my cousin's *oyfruf*.

These and other incidents nevertheless were quietly put behind me. They didn't total up to anything, and they certainly were not enough to shake my equilibrium.

And then came feminism. In 1963, I read Betty Friedan's *Feminine Mystique*, still the classic text of the women's movement. I was a little intimidated by its force and had trouble with what seemed to me a portent of friction between the sexes, but the essential idea, equality of women, was exciting, mind-boggling, and very just. Still, correct or not, it didn't mean me, nor did it apply to women in Judaism. On that score I was defensive, resistant, and probably just plain frightened. It must have threatened my status quo.

And yet . . . Once I had tasted of the fruit of the tree of knowledge, there was no going back. The basic idea had found a resting spot somewhere inside me. Little by little, and with a good deal of prodding from my husband, I became sensitized to issues and situations that previously had made no impression on me. Some of my complacency was eroded; my placidity churned up. In place of blind acceptance, I slowly began to ask questions, not really sure if I wanted to hear the answers. Because I was so satisfied, because I had no sense of injustice, some of the new thinking, including my own, came to me as a shock. Things that had run right past me before I now had to grab hold of, for a still moment, to examine under the white light of equality.

I began to think not just about the idea, but about myself as a woman—in relation to people, to a place in the larger society, to a career, and finally to Judaism. I did not look back over my past and say it was bad. In fact, I knew it was very good. What I did begin to say was that perhaps it could have been better. Again, it was not a case of closing my eyes and thinking hard. Instead, it was a series of incidents, encounters, a matter of timing; it was also memories and recollections, a review in which isolated incidents began to emerge as part of a pattern. This pattern now had to be tested against a new value framework.

It was almost ten years before I began systematically to apply the new categories to my Jewishness. As I reviewed my education, one fact emerged—a fact so obvious that I was stunned more by my unresponsiveness to it over the years than by the fact itself. It was this: the study of Talmud, which was a primary goal in my family and community, consistently was closed off to me. Beginning with elementary school, the girls studied Israeli folk dancing while the boys studied Talmud. In the yeshiva high school, the girls' branch had no course of study in Talmud; the boys' branch had three hours a day. In Israel, in the Jewish studies seminar, all of the classes were coeducational except Talmud. The girls studied laws and customs on one day and enjoyed a free period the other four days.

And then there was my father. The great love of his life, beyond his family, was not his business; it was his study of the Talmud. Every day, before he left for work, he would spend an hour studying Talmud with a rabbi friend. In fact, he has not missed a day of study in his life, even during family vacations or times of stress. Yet although he reviewed religious texts regularly with his daughters, it was never Talmud. He even would collar my dates, while I was getting ready, for a few minutes of Talmud discussion. That we didn't participate in those years more directly in our father's passion for Talmud study was not a willful denial on his part; he simply was following the hallowed custom. As a result of all this, when I began to study rabbinic literature in graduate school in my late twenties, I realized that my male fellow students all had the edge of fifteen or twenty years of Talmud study behind them.

Gradually, too, I became aware of the power of conditioning and how early in life it takes place. On the last Sabbath that my husband served as rabbi of a congregation, the children and I decided to surprise him. Moshe, then ten and a half, prepared the haftarah reading, David, nine, the *An'im Zemirot* prayer, and J.J., six, the *Adon Olam*. It was a real treat for their father and for the entire congregation; it seemed to the boys as if the whole world was proud of them. On the following Sunday morning, their grandparents visited and gave each of the boys two dollars for doing such a fine job. When the boys told Deborah, then eight, that they each had been given two dollars, she complained that it wasn't fair. At which point Moshe retorted, with the biting honesty of a ten year old: "Well, so what, you can't even do anything in the synagogue!" Click, click, I thought to myself, another woman radicalized.

Oddly enough, until that moment it never had occurred to me that it could or should be otherwise, that perhaps it wasn't "fair" to a little girl. Even more astounding was the fact that with all the weeks of secret practice, all the fuss I had made over the boys beforehand, and all the compliments they received afterward, Deborah never once had complained. It was only the two dollars that finally got to her; to everything else she had already been conditioned . . . to expect nothing.

Other scenes began to pull together. When my Uncle Izzie died, the whole family gathered for his funeral. He had been a cheerful, expansive man, much beloved by everyone. He had had a special spot in his heart for his six grandchildren, especially two girls who grew up in his house. In his eulogy, the rabbi commented on this special relationship. At the end of the service, he asked the grandchildren to accompany the casket out of the synagogue. Three boys and three girls, all in their teens, stepped forward. The president of the congregation hastened over and asked the girls to be seated. The rabbi, he said, meant only male grandchildren.

A few months later, my husband and I went to visit a friend and her daughter who were observing shivah, the seven-day mourning period. We arrived just in time for the evening service. The men rose to pray. The women, including the two mourners, were shunted off to the apartment foyer to stand silently while the men prayed. The men who had arranged the service did not think to provide prayer books for the women, not even for the two female mourners. Nor did it occur to them to move to the foyer themselves at least to allow the women to remain seated in the living room. It was as if once the moment of prayer began, the women no longer existed. None of the men present could be characterized as ill-mannered; each was considerate of women and all were solicitous of the two mourners, the wife and daughter of the deceased. Yet as I stood in my tight corner of the foyer, I recalled a picture I once had seen of Muslim women with their babies, shunted into a similar position, and inwardly I wondered at how smug I had been then.

A turning point for me came in 1973. By sheer accident I was invited to deliver the opening address at the First National Jewish Women's Conference, to be held at the Hotel McAlpin in New York. A month before the conference, two young women, Arlene Agus and Toby Brandriss, came to our house to discuss the conference and to invite my husband to participate in a Sunday morning panel. As we chatted, I chimed in intermittently. Several times I had to leave the room to attend to the children. At one point I went off to put our daughter Goody, then six, to bed. As is the prescribed custom before retiring for the night, Goody got ready to recite the *Shema Yisrael* prayer. A few days earlier we had bought the latest record of the Israeli Hasidic folk festival, which contained a lovely new melody for the *Shema*, quite different from the version we were used to singing at bedtime. When I tucked Goody in, I sang the *Shema* with her to the new tune. Then, just as I was about to leave the room, she said softly, "Now can we say the real *Shema*?" Moments later, I recounted the story to our visitors and added with laughter, "Here you have it, a case in point of why it's going to be so tough to get anywhere with those new ideas of yours." Their response took me by surprise. "Say," said one of the visitors with utter spontaneity, "how would *you* like to speak at the opening session on Friday night with Dr. S. [a well-known woman speaker]?" The next day Toby and Arlene called and with some embarrassment reported that Dr. S. did not want to share the platform, certainly not with a neophyte like me; would I mind giving a workshop instead? "Fine," I said. Two weeks later they called again. The woman had decided to cancel altogether; would I give the opening address? It was definitely a case of being in the right place at the right time.

Until then I had thought through the Jewish issues of feminism only haphazardly—in the shower, watching people, daydreaming in the synagogue or at school, reflecting on the relevant items I came across in the classic Jewish sources, and vaguely relating bits of all this to my own experience. Now I was forced to collect my scattered thought, to research, to focus. When I confronted the sources directly, I found I could no longer accept the apologetic line so popular among those in the traditional Jewish community who were attempting to deal with feminism. Different role assignments? Yes, that part was true. But genuine equality? There was simply too much evidence to the contrary. On the other hand, my background, indeed my love for the tradition, had given me a different perspective on the feminist movement. Untempered, it seemed to me, feminism fell short in some basic human values. Thus, as my talk developed, it ended up being a double-edged critique of Jewish tradition vis-à-vis women and feminism, each from a perspective of the other.

The response was most instructive. I discovered that there were some feminists who relished criticism of the Jewish tradition but would brook no naysaying of feminism. They applauded the first part of my address and hissed at the second part. In my later conversations with them, and in my observations throughout the weekend, I began to realize that it was their counterparts in the broader feminist movement (about whom I had been reading) who had given me pause. I thought of them as "orthodox" feminists, for feminism was to them a religion—sacrosanct, untouchable, inviolable. They were the vociferous minority, the radical fringe, whom the self-serving media had projected to the center, passing up the more balanced, less angry elements of the movement. Perhaps the radical fringe is a necessary leaven in any bloodless revolution, but it was also a lesson for me to realize how deeply this fringe could discredit the very movement it held up as ideal. This was an important encounter for me. After that weekend, I found myself less in need of prefacing my comments on the subject with such remarks as "I'm not a women's libber." I found you could still be a mild-mannered yeshiva girl and a card-carrying feminist and not feel out of whack all the time.

More significant was the conference experience itself and the larger group that was present. To my amazement, there were some five hundred women from every point along the continuum, not just the twenty-five hard-core types I had expected to find. Although all were feminists, they were not hostile to Judaism. A good many of them, especially those with no extensive Jewish background, had come to Judaism through feminism: in the course of searching for their roots as women, they had begun to search for their roots as Jews. The tone was not as I had feared, a shrill, seventy-two-hour tirade against Jewish tradition. Instead, the whole weekend abounded with a great deal of love for Judaism.

Moreover, as I looked about me, I was astonished to see what the conference organizers—a handful of women in their twenties, inexperienced volunteers for the most part—had achieved: a smooth-running, well-synchronized, rich program with something of value for everyone. I was teaching then at a college that had been founded and successfully run by women, but I had thought that only starched nuns or super-efficient Hadassah ladies could pull off something so professional, so successful. It was a striking lesson in women's initiative.

From the conference, I began to understand the value of cohorts, the strength one derives from a like-minded community—the support, the testing of ideas, the cross-fertilization. Until then, except for conversations with my husband, the process for me had been a very private one.

I learned to relax, not to be so rigid when it came to women's experimentation with new responsibilities. I had heard there would be a women's minyan during the course of the conference. Naturally, I wouldn't participate! The first minyan was held on Friday night prior to the formal opening of the conference, when I was to deliver the keynote address. I prayed alone in my room, feeling on the one hand quite self-righteous and, on the other, secure in the knowledge that since I knew only two or three people there, no one would notice my absence. By Saturday morning, however, I was a known quantity, and to stay away from the services would have been conspicuous. So very hesitantly I brought myself down to the women's minyan and sat as far back in the room as I could. I was astounded to hear a woman leading the prayers. Next came another surprise—a woman's melodious voice reading the Torah with the perfect cantillation. Somehow, I had thought that only thirteen-year-old boys were equal to the task. I found it very beautiful.

Finally, there came the real shocker. After the Torah reading, I saw two women, acting in the capacity of gabbaim (synagogue officials), coming down the center aisle toward the back where I was sitting. The last thing in the world I wanted was a synagogue honor. I prayed silently, "Please, don't let it be me." Sure enough, they had come to invite me to step forward for the honor of *hagba'ah* (the raising up of the Torah before it is returned to the ark). Choose someone else, I pleaded. They persisted gently but firmly. It was only good breeding that propelled me down the aisle. Then something happened that was to make me think for a long time about the value of practiced skills. I had seen *hagba'ah* performed at least a thousand times in my life. Yet, as I stood there, I had to ask the woman standing next to me, "What do I do now?" Also, to my surprise, caught as I was with my defenses down, I found it an exhilarating moment. It was the first time I had ever held a Torah scroll.

After the conference, I began to think more seriously and to read some of the Jewish feminist literature that had been around for years but that I, in my private putterings, somehow had missed. I came across an article written two years earlier by Rachel Adler that is still one of the finest and most succinct statements I have read on Jewish feminism, and one by Trude Weiss-Rosmarin written as far back as 1969 that dealt cogently with some of the central problems we are still concerned with today. Little by little, I was able to examine what the other Jewish denominations were doing, without ruling something out just because Conservative or Reform or Reconstructionist Judaism had got there first.

Still, it wasn't a smooth path. Like millions of other women and men, I've pretty much stumbled my way through this revolution. Perhaps because the divisions were so clear and sharp and well defined, I often felt an emotional resistance to things I could accept on a theoretical level. Partly because the lines were so heavily drawn, I found it difficult to know what is form and what is essence in the traditional dichotomy between male and female. It was even more difficult to understand that at certain points in a normative religion, form and essence are one and the same—but who can know these intersecting points?

In 1973, I was still able to say, "Women in the Reform rabbinate, that's one thing. As for Orthodox me, I'll take my rabbis male, thank you." The first time I saw a woman draped in a prayer shawl, my instinctive reaction was, *am ha'aretz*, ignoramus. The first time I spotted a young woman wearing a *kipah* in the library of the Jewish Theological Seminary, I thought she was spoofing; it never occurred to me she might be in earnest. As I drew nearer and saw her studying Mishnah, I began to feel a charge of anxiety. For the rest of the morning I couldn't concentrate on my own work. Instead, I tried to figure out what she was doing under that powder-blue *kipah*. And I tried to figure out why I was so uneasy. Was it because, once again, someone had crossed the lines? I know what my reaction will be on that day when I see some smart-aleck woman marching around with tzitzit—the ritual fringes worn by observant Jewish males—hanging out. Maybe, if she's not some kind of exhibitionist but rather a deeply religious Jew, eventually I'll overcome my palpitations and begin to consider what kind of statement she is making. Maybe I'll even have to consider the possibility that my own great-granddaughters will be obligated to wear some equivalent of tzitzit.

Sometimes I found myself switching gears from one moment to the next. One evening, as I sat in a graduate rabbinic literature course, the professor departed from his explication of the text at hand to comment on an article that had appeared that morning on the front page of the *New York Times* about the Conservative movement's decision to count women in a minyan. "This Jew," he said, in a tone not quite free of derision, "gets up in the morning. His five children start to get up, and all at once the house is in an uproar. Now he sets off to the synagogue for the early morning minyan. By the time he gets home, his wife has the children washed, dressed, fed, and off to school. The house is quiet again and he sits down to a peaceful breakfast and an hour of leisurely study. When he comes back in the evening from work, the place is an uproar again. So he takes his prayer book and his Bible and goes off to the synagogue again. Now I ask you, what's he going to do if his good wife has to go to the minyan?" This account was greeted by a sustained roar of knowing laughter.

In the classroom at that moment were fourteen yeshiva men— half of them rabbis, the rest preparing for ordination—and me. I laughed along with everyone else, but after three seconds I said to myself, "Why am I laughing?" Was this not a case of how the primal association of men with synagogue as male refuge and women with home and family was communicated, ever so subtly, from one generation to the next? Not wishing to jeopardize my standing in the group and their gracious acceptance of me, I said nothing. I watched as they laughed along without me. Aware of what had passed at that moment, I began to wonder whether the core issue here had to do with Orthodox versus Conservative, as it seemed, or, on a much deeper level, a matter of male versus female. Or was it both, the two inextricably intertwined? And if so, where did that leave me?

I began to discern that just as I was becoming more open and less anxious about my feminist impulses, there were many in the community who were tightening up and closing off. Some of the issues were political as well as religious. In 1976, for instance, my own synagogue was deciding whether to allow women a member-ship vote. Several women asked me what the rule was in other synagogues. I had no idea, so I undertook an unscientific survey and called ten Orthodox synagogues in the New York area. About one-third of them allowed women to vote; one even had a woman vice-president. In one case, the associate rabbi told me that women could not vote, but then again, he added, neither could the men; synagogue affairs here were the preserve of a three-man oligarchy. At another synagogue the secretary would not put me through to the rabbi. When she heard what I was calling about, she retorted, "Of course women don't vote here; it's against the Torah. You can't bother the rabbi with such foolish questions." At a third synagogue, the cheery sexton who took my call replied, "When women come to the 7:00 A.M. minyan, I'll give them the vote."

I didn't ask him whether he applied that rule to all the voting members of the synagogue; I already knew the answer.

I found certain other issues quite offensive, too, such as the discussion over the rabbinic precept *kol ishah ervah* ("a woman's voice leads to licentiousness," implying that women may not sing in the presence of men). *Kol ishah* had not been a popular theme in Orthodoxy in the fifties and sixties; if the precept had any religious redeeming value, it clearly escaped me. I half suspected that *kol ishah* was dredged up in the seventies as a counterpoint to women's new freedom of expression, and I openly debated the issue as the need arose. To me, *kol ishah* seemed nothing but an overt slur on the female sex, an arbitrary curb on women in the name of a one-sided modesty meter. Could this be the mild-mannered yeshiva girl speaking?

For me, at least, the process is not over, this interweaving of feminism and Judaism. Because one is continuously exposed to those encounters and incidents that affect one's worldview, I suspect I will have ample occasion to go through several more cycles of thought and feeling before it all stabilizes. I intend to keep my eyes wide open, watching to see what works and what doesn't, what is viable within the framework of Jewish tradition and what isn't. I hope to gain a clearer picture of where the lines should be drawn, which respected authorities should draw them, and where to push further.

Two things I know for sure. My questioning never will lead me to abandon tradition. I am part of a chain that is too strong to break, and though it needs no protection from me, a child of the tradition, I want to protect it with the fierceness of a mother protecting her young. But I also know that I never can yield the new value of women's equality, even though it may conflict with Jewish tradition. To do so would be to affirm the principle of a hierarchy of male and female, and this I no longer believe to be an axiom of Judaism.

I feel instinctively that drawing the lines is important and correct at both fundamental and transcendental levels. Divisions of labor and function are, in fact, humanly expedient; there is a remarkable staying power of sexual identity and distinctiveness, the uniqueness of male and female beyond biology. Yet there are many instances in which the sex-role divisions in Judaism do not work. To deny participation in this or that experience because one is a man or a woman is an act of inhumanity. Somehow, Judaism will have to find a way to bridge the gap.

Meanwhile, there is probably a great deal of tension in store for people like me. But that no longer frightens me, neither personally nor in terms of the system. In fact, I suspect—indeed, I know— that ultimately Judaism will emerge stronger and not weaker from this encounter with feminism. Happiness for a mild-mannered yeshiva girl? Less naiveté perhaps, more unrest, a constant prob- ing, endless queries. Surely that's no blueprint for happiness. But the engagement of Judaism and feminism offers something else: new heights to scale, a deeper sense of maturity, and an enlarged scope of responsibility for oneself, society, and the continuity of tradition—exactly what the religious endeavor is all about.

The Theoretical Basis of
Women's Equality in Judaism

I

WE who are committed to traditional Judaism are standing today at the crossroads on the question of women. Feminism disturbs our previous equilibrium, for it makes a fundamental claim about women contrary to the model generated by Halakhah.

The feminist ideology can be summed up as follows:

1. Women have the same innate potential, capability, and needs as men, whether in the realm of the spirit, the word, or the deed.
2. Women have a similar capacity for interpretation and concomitant decision making.
3. Women can function fully as "outside" persons, in broader areas of society beyond the home.
4. Women can and should have some control over their own destinies, to the extent that such mastery is possible for anyone.

Let us reduce these broad statements from the level of generalization to a theology of woman as Jew:

1. A woman of faith has the same innate vision and existential longing for a redemptive-covenantal reality as a man of faith.[1] She has the same ability and need to be in the presence of God alone and within the context of the community. Such a woman is sufficiently mature to accept the responsibilities for this relationship and the rights that flow from these responsibilities. If these spiritual gifts do not flow naturally from her soul, she can be educated and uplifted in them in much the same fashion that Jewish men are.

2. Jewish women, as much as men, have the mental and emotional capacities to deal directly with the most sacred Jewish texts and primary sources. Jewish women are capable of interpreting tradition based on the sources. They can be involved in the decision-making process that grows out of the blending of inherited tradition with contemporary needs.

3. Some women, as some men, are capable of functioning in the positions of authority related to the religious and physical survival of the Jewish people.

4. Women as a class should not find themselves in discriminatory positions in personal situations. In such matters as marriage and divorce, a woman should have no less control or personal freedom than a man, nor should she be subject to abuse resulting from the constriction of freedom.

These, then, are the basic claims that a woman, sensitized to the new, broader, cultural value system, can carry over into her life as a Jew. I am not arguing here whether halakhic Judaism deems a woman inferior, although there are more than a few sources in the tradition that lend themselves to such a conclusion;[2] nor will I accept at face value those statements that place women on a separate but higher pedestal. What I am saying is that Halakhah, contrary to the feminist values I have described above, continues to delimit women. In some very real ways, halakhic parameters inhibit women's growth, both as Jews and as human beings.

I do not speak here of all of Halakhah. One must be careful not to generalize from certain critical comments and apply them to the system as a whole. In fact, my critique could grow only out of a profound appreciation for the system in its entirety—its ability to preserve the essence of an ancient revelation as a fresh experience each day; its power to generate an abiding sense of kinship, past and present; its intimate relatedness to concerns both immediate and other-wordly; its psychological soundness; its ethical and moral integrity. On the whole, I believe that a Jew has a better chance of living a worthwhile life if he or she lives a life according to Halakhah. Therefore, I do not feel threatened when addressing the question of the new needs of women in Judaism nor in admitting the limitations of Halakhah in this area. Indeed, it is my very faith in halakhic Judaism that makes me believe we can search within it for a new level of perfection, as Jews have been doing for three thousand years.

From this understanding one is moved perforce to ask the next question: if the new feminist categories are perceived to be of a higher order of definition of woman than those that limit her, how are we to explain the gap between the feminist model and the halakhic model? This becomes even more problematic when one considers the sheer abundance of ethical and moral constructs in Judaism (e.g., the injunctions not to insult another, to lift up one's brother before he falls, not to lead another into temptation, not to judge unless one has been faced with the same situation). How is it possible that a tradition with so highly developed a sensitivity to human beings could allow even one law or value judgment that demeans women, much less a host of such laws?

There are certain external and internal factors that explain the insufficiency of the tradition with regard to women. The stratification of men and women in Judaism simply reflects the male-female hierarchical status in all previous societies in human history.[3] Moreover, in light of the primary model of Jewish woman as domestic creature—as wife, mother, dependent, auxiliary—all other roles and responsibilities that seemed to conflict with the primary model simply were eliminated.[4]

I do not wish to imply that Jewish women were oppressed. This is far from the truth. Given the historically universal stratification of the sexes, plus the model of the Jewish woman as enabler and the exclusive male (rabbinic) option of interpreting the law, there could have been widespread abuse of the powerless. But this did not happen. In fact, the reverse is true; throughout rabbinic history, one observes a remarkably benign and caring attitude toward women.

Nevertheless, there is a need today to redefine the status of women in certain areas of Jewish law. First, a benign and caring stance is not discernible in every last instance of rabbinic legislation.[5] Second, paternalism is not what women are seeking nowadays, not even the women of the traditional Jewish community. Increasingly, such women are beginning to ask questions about equality, about a more mature sharing of responsibility, about divesting the power of halakhic interpretation and legislation of its singular maleness.

II

I have referred to the crossroads at which we stand. A crossroad implies choices. There are three ways in which halakhic Jews may proceed with regard to the question of women:

1. We can revert to the fundamentalist pole, where hierarchy of male and female remains unchallenged in most areas of human life.
2. We can allow the new value system to penetrate our civil lives but not our religious lives. In other words, women may be encouraged to see themselves as equals in social, economic, and political spheres. This is the current stance of modern Orthodoxy.
3. We can find ways within Halakhah to allow for growth and greater equality in the ritual and spiritual realms, despite the fact that there are no guarantees where this will lead us.

It is my firm belief that the third path is the one we now must begin to follow. Admittedly, I have been propelled in that direction by the contemporary Western humanist liberation philosophy of the secular women's movement; those who would hurl at me the charge of "foreign-body contamination" therefore are absolutely right. But is there any religion in history, including Judaism, that has not borrowed from the surrounding culture? The real question is, What do we do with what we borrow? What are the unique Jewish ways in which we appropriate positive ideas, customs, and values? How we can enhance our system by these new accretions? And most important, in what ways can they become continuous with the essence of Judaism?

True, the original impulse for all this, as I have said, derives from feminism, but even if such a movement hadn't evolved, I still would like to think that a creative pondering of the ideals of Torah Judaism might lead to the same conclusions. Thus, the central concern of these observations has to do with organic, internal changes, changes in our private Jewish lives, unmediated by society, quotas, affirmative action, and the like—changes based on intrinsic Jewish values and brought about because the halakhic way of life calls them forth.

III

Let us examine briefly some working principles of Halakhah. Halakhah is not simply a collection of laws. It is a way of life or, more correctly, a way of living. For a Jew, a life directed by Halakhah is as near perfect a way of life as possible. The sum of its parts—observing the Sabbath, kashrut, giving to charity, having a family, being part of a community, teaching children, studying Torah, loving God—is infinitely greater than each of the parts. All things great and small—reciting a blessing over new clothes, or after elimination, or over different varieties of foods; cutting the toenails, or breaking an egg the Jewish way—each minute act further distills that Jewish core.

Why do I say "near perfect"? Halakhah is a system that is being perfected continually. Indeed, the rabbinic tradition stresses humanity's role as a partner in the task of perfecting an imperfect world. One cannot but perceive Halakhah as a fluid, dynamic system. Fluidity on specific laws about women is itself an example of that dynamism.

Halakhah interprets and reflects reality, not just tradition. Halakhah never operated in a totally closed system. There always has been a healthy consideration of immediate circumstances and broader societal forces. Even when rabbinic leaders enacted circumscribing legislation, that too was a form of interaction with broader society. The whole body of responsa literature reflects those influences. So do such rabbinic concepts as *gezerah she-ayn ha-tzibur yakhol la-amod bah* ("restrictions imposed upon the populace that the majority cannot endure are not to be levied") and *dina de-malkhuta dina* ("the civil law of the land is the law").

The techniques of reinterpretation are built right into the system. It was proper use of these techniques that enabled rabbinic Judaism to be continuous with the past, even as it redefined and redirected the present and future. The techniques also allowed for diversity, for allowances based on local usage, for a certain kind of pluralism. After all, in a normative system how can you have two ways of doing something without each side's reading the other out of the community? Hence, the acceptance of various *minhagim* (customs). Once a particular *minhag* withstood the test of time, it became an integral part of Halakhah.

An even more striking example of the technique of halakhic accommodation is the use of *asmakhta*, a scriptural passage or word on which a novel transition is pegged. An *asmakhta* often seems illogical, farfetched, arbitrary. Yet the logic is in the technique itself. Through the use of *asmakhta* one never loses sight of the original revelation at Sinai, even though the new interpretation may go far beyond the old. Other halakhic techniques to accomplish similar ends are takkanot (directives enacted by halakhic scholars enjoying the force of law), *gezerot* (precautionary rulings), and *hora'at sha'ah* (emergency rulings); even pilpulistic interpretations were used to develop and refine legal rulings further.

A central theme seems to emerge: where there was a rabbinic will, there was a halakhic way. This is not to say that talmudic and post-talmudic literature is not "the law of Moses at Sinai." It is that, but it is also the substance of rabbinic will finding a halakhic way. What shall we call it? Continuing revelation? Wise, interpretive judgment based on inherited tradition? An understanding, divinely given or intuited, of the appropriate moment for greater restraint, or relaxation of the rules, or heightened responsibility? Surely the rabbinic decision to accept the testimony of a wife or a single witness—as sufficient evidence to establish the fact of death of the husband and thereby free her to remarry—is a sign of rabbinic compassion that somehow found halakhic expression. Surely Rabbenu Gershom, the tenth-century authority, used his power and position to enact a takkanah (ordinance) that disallowed forcible divorce.

A good deal of leeway in interpretation was given to individual scholars. The lack of centralization of authority from the Second Temple period and onward was not perceived as a weakness in rabbinic tradition. The concept of *moreh de-atra* (following the ruling of the local rabbinic authority), the full disclosure of disputes between scholars, the transmission of minority ruling along with the majority ones—these are as fundamental to the workings of Torah as Torah itself.

There is a heavy emphasis of ethical content in biblical and rabbinic literature. Ethical principles are at least as important as ritual ones.[6] The concept of equality in both ethical and ritual spheres emerges not only as principle but as process—a gradual movement from a society where slavery was permitted to the de facto abolishment of slavery; the jubilee year as a means of avoiding concentration of wealth in the hands of a few; the developing structure of a convenantal community rather than a hierarchical one; authority based on merit (the rabbis) rather than birth or wealth (priests, Levites, and landowners). Clearly, this trend in Jewish history—hierarchial to covenantal, birth to merit—has far-reaching implications for women in Judaism.

IV

In light of these working principles of Halakhah, one must ask some pointed questions: Does halakhic stratification of the sexes explicitly serve a theological purpose, that is, relatedness to God? For example, is inequity in divorce law or exclusion from court testimony or insufficiency to be counted for a quorum of some ultimate value in Judaism? Is there any way that the release of women from the obligation to study Torah, or praying at the prescribed times, can be understood in the sense of *kedushah*, holiness, a "setting aside"? We are offered no reasons for observing kashrut, yet we clearly understand it as an act of holiness, a special calling, a symbol of the unique relationship between God and the Jewish people. Is that how we must understand the stratification of male and female in Jewish ritual? Must we say that God's eternal plan for the sexes was a hierarchy, one dominant and one subordinate sex as law and ritual define us? Could it be that God, who loves all of His creatures, prefers and esteems the devotion of one whole class more than the other? Or can we say perhaps that the inequity is reflective of an undisputed socioreligious stance of ancient times?

Intuitively, and with a new awareness of the ethics of male-female equality, I find it hard to accept any notion that assigns to God a plan for hierarchy of the sexes: role division, yes to some extent; but superiority, no. That could be only a time-bound, human interpretation of God's will, from which women ought now to be exempt. If the male-female stratification is sociological rather than theological, are we bound to it forever? Does the fact that this long-standing sociological truth has been codified into Halakhah oblige us to make an eternal principle out of an accident of history? For that answer we must turn to other characteristics of the Halakhah, as I have indicated above: its proven ability to undergo reinterpretation in specific areas, particularly on women's issues; its pattern of equalizing unequals; its allowance for human subjectivity; its process of self-perfection over the long course of its unfolding; its emphasis on ethical sensitivity so that no class of people feels disadvantaged; its movement from ascribed to earned status, with authority flowing from merit, not birth or sex.

It would seem, then, that full equalization of women in Judaism should be consistent with the wider principles of Torah. In fact, we ought to go one step further. If the hierarchy of the sexes serves no religious function, if Halakhah has the capacity for reinterpretation, if equality is a basic positive value in Judaism, then it behooves the community and its leaders to take the initiative; together they must search for new ways to upgrade religious expression and new means by which to generate equality for women in tradition. No longer shall we hear the argument that women are demanding this or that of the Halakhah. Rather, the issue should be set forth in the following terms: Halakhah, the Jewish way, cries out for reinterpretation in the light of the new awareness of feminine equality, feminine potential.

V

Let us apply this theoretical structure to specific situations. Given the unmistakable pattern toward equalization in Jewish divorce law—that is, the gradual limitation of the male's absolute rights and the gradual expansion of protections for women—the rabbis of today can no longer plead an inability to rectify the inequity. To say that their hands are tied or that they can resolve an individual case but cannot find a comprehensive solution is to admit that they are unworthy of the authority vested in them. Worse, it bespeaks a lack of rabbinic will to find a halakhic way. How else is one to explain the reluctance of certain *gedolim* (rabbinic authorities) to build upon the halakhic groundwork laid out by such contemporary scholars as Emanuel Rackman, Eliezer Berkovits, and Ze'ev Falk, who have come forth with alternative solutions in the form of respectable halakhic precedents? What these *gedolim*, the principal religious decision makers of contemporary Orthodoxy, are really saying is that they feel a need to preserve the original male prerogative in matters of divorce, for they know well that the only person whose hands are tied is the woman, who is often fair game for blackmail.

Similarly, we can apply the theoretical model to education and religious leadership. If Torah study and its teaching is something of high value, surpassing all other mitzvot, what could possibly justify closing off parts of the activity to one half of our people? Is it ethical to say that women are unequal to the task, especially when exceptional models have indicated otherwise? Moreover, here is a clear instance whereby the system continuously perfects itself. What is accepted now in the way of Torah study for women was absolutely out of bounds three generations ago. Sarah Schneier, the founder of the Bais Yaakov movement of education for girls, faced severe opposition in her time, but every young Jewish woman who has received a Jewish education from that day on is the beneficiary of her vision and persistence. Once she accomplished what she did, those who watched it happen and those who understood it as a more perfect expression of a woman's Jewishness somehow found a halakhic way to make Jewish education for women legitimate, even desirable.

Let us press the perfection model one step further and confront the dilemma head on. If the study of Torah and Mishnah is not forbidden to women, why does Talmud remain off limits? And if certain study is permitted to women, why is it not encouraged? The answer is clear: because direct access to learning is the key to religious leadership in the traditional Jewish community. Without it, there is no way a woman can qualify as a scholar, a halakhic decision maker, or a rabbi. With equal access, women will begin to raise disturbing questions. A woman with a sense of her innate potential will begin to ask, "Why shouldn't I, too, strive to be learned?" A woman the match in learning of any rabbinical student will sooner or later ask, "Why can't I, too, be ordained?" Ultimately, a new generation of parents who place high value on Torah study will ask, "Why not expect the same from our daughters as from our sons?"

To deny fulfillment of these expectations is to assume that women never can be equal to men in spirit and intellect and therefore to demean and shame the class of women; it is also to deny Halakhah its power to interpret reality—and live. If it is none of these things, then it can be only a means of reserving power and authority as an exclusively male prerogative. Otherwise, who would not share Torah with all who seek it.

Finally, we come to a consideration of the place of women in Jewish liturgy. If prayer is a form of Jewish commitment, if women as Jews are nourished by the same covenantal-redemptive vision, how can we justify excluding them from the unity of the spiritual congregation? Some would advance the familiar set of hoary arguments—that the honor of the community is diminished by women's participation, that women are not capable of making a sustained commitment to the fixed times of prayer, that women are unable to handle the tension between this pull and that. But are these real descriptions of a whole class of women? Were they ever inherent truths, or simply convenient excuses to preserve the privileges of a male fraternity whose business, admirably enough, was God-centered?

If one perceives that change of any sort goes against the grain of the Halakhah, then there can be no shared universe of discourse above the level of form. If, on the other hand, we begin with the idea of Halakhah as the divine way to perfection, then we can proceed to examine form and essence independently. If prayer (essence) is primary in the Jewish system and fraternity (form) secondary, the next stage would be to acknowledge women as equals in the spiritual community and allow men to find other expression for their fraternal impulses.

A sense of community emanates not so much from shared physical presence as from shared memory and obligation. Thus, a Jew experiences feelings of kinship even when praying in the privacy of his home. The inclusion of women in liturgy—public and private —becomes, then, a building up of tradition and community, not a breaking down. If young boys can grow biologically into Jewish responsibilities, perhaps it is not too much to expect that women can grow historically.

VI

So much for an idealized rendering of Jewish feminism. Despite the fact that the theory seems to fit—internally consistent, organically linked, and halakhically coherent—there remains nevertheless much fear and resistance, the kind that goes far beyond learned considerations.

The antagonists' charges take many forms: tampering with Halakhah, changing the unchangeable, watering down Judaism, undermining the family, destroying virtues of female modesty, blurring sexual roles, mixing religion with sexual politics. And finally the veiled and distant threat that while these specific emendations in Halakhah in and of themselves may be fine, all this tinkering ultimately will undermine Torah, tradition, mitzvot, Halakhah, norms, faith, stability, rootedness; in short, everything we hold so dear.

This is indeed a heavy load for Jewish feminists to bear. Surely some of the voiced fears serve to prevent those with new ideas from veering too widely off course. Nevertheless, these fears must be addressed directly, for they have a way of escalating, of feeding on themselves, of losing touch with reality.

One aspect of that reality is that the status quo, as we have inherited it, has not been totally static. Surely there are risks involved whenever tradition undergoes change. But Halakhah is not to be treated as a *goses*, a rapidly failing body that one cannot move lest it give out its final death rattle. Halakhah was intended to be preserved, and there is a healthy difference between preserving and freezing solid. "Preserving" does not preclude bringing to the system human responses that will enhance and expand Torah values. Those who counter this claim with labels of Conservative and Reform are simply playing the name game, an easy way to avoid confronting the issues.

Taking the risk at its very worst, if giving religious equality to women should turn out to be a dreadful mistake for ritual life, there ought to be that recognition and assurance that halakhic Judaism will outlast the folly of any single generation. To think otherwise bespeaks a lack of faith in the divinity, as well as the eternality, of Revelation and the Covenant. It also bespeaks an overwhelming pride and cosmic immodesty to assume that the entire religious enterprise depends wholly on human action or inaction.

Let us now turn to the accusation that these adaptations constitute a watering down of Judaism. I find myself thoroughly confused by this equation, even more so when I hear its paraphrase: "Strike a blow for Yiddishkeit, keep a woman from learning Torah." Does the encouragement of women's learning or the inclusion of women in the prayer structure actually sap the strength of Judaism?

If the religious community operates by the criteria that guided us throughout rabbinic history, then this accusation must fly out the window. We must ask the proper questions: Do the changes enable us to grow as Jews? Do they enlarge our commitment in some way? Are they serious and sustained additions to the religious life? Certainly an increase of obligations and rights for women cannot be equated to adding a fifth fringe on the tzitzit or a fifth variety to the lulav.[7]

The charge that Jewish feminists are mixing religion with sexual politics must be examined, not denied. Those who say it is unthinkable, unwise, unholy, or untraditional to speak of Halakhah and political pressure in the same breath are simply hiding historical facts. Politics and pressure—the substance as well as the art— certainly have affected halakhic decisions throughout our history. How could leaders know the needs of individuals and special interest groups if not through politics, pressure, power plays, protest, and pleading. These actions enabled those with knowledge and authority to bring a different subjectivity to their task of interpreting the law.

The issue of *tzniut* has often been invoked in discussions of such matters. (*Tzniut* is the concept that embraces privacy, modesty, restraint, decency, and chasteness.) Is there a loss of this virtue as women take on public and private roles previously assigned only to men? Yes, if we define *tzniut* to mean women as "inside" persons with no public presence in ritual or liturgy and subject to circumscribed actions and areas of control; breaking all these taboos, in this view, constitutes a flagrant violation of the norms of *tzniut*. But it is necessary to define *tzniut* of women more broadly, that is, in terms of its characteristics, not its role limits. *Tzniut* is both absolute and relative; absolute in modes of behavior, dress, speech, and relative in all those things as well. In certain communities at certain times, a woman did not initiate actions, speak until spoken to, or venture forth into public places (a man's domain); she did not uncover her ankles, elbows, neck, eyes. What is today perfectly acceptable behavior in the modern Orthodox community in speech, thought, dress, and action was unheard of a generation ago. Furthermore, what is permissible in one community is not permitted in another.

At a recent conference in Israel, held at a religious kibbutz, not a single Israeli woman, not even the *shaitl*-covered wives of some of the yeshiva rabbis, wore nylon stockings at the Sabbath synagogue services. Sandal-covered feet were considered modest enough; not so the American women present, who wouldn't think of showing up in shul with bare toes. And at a recent *sheva berakhot*—a celebration in honor of the newly married couple—the young bride, a graduate of the strict Orthodox Bais Yaakov school, delivered a *d'var Torah* (homily) in the mixed audience. This would have been considered *peritzut* (licentious behavior) a mere generation ago.

Even in the most closed sectors of the Jewish community, women are no longer inside persons. They are moving inexorably in the other direction, into jobs, careers, higher education, communal roles. A woman who assumes a public presence in secular society without overstepping the bounds of an internal modesty will do no less in the religious sector. To enable a woman to become a bat Torah is hardly likely to lead her to immorality; to consider a woman part of the holy congregation will not lead to profligacy. Initially, the newness of it all may jar the sensibilities, but soon much of it will be taken for granted. With hindsight, we shall say how inadequate our double standards were.

All of this is not to discard *tzniut* as a criterion of behavior for men as well as women, in secular as well as religious life. Surely there is too little of it today; Western social mores have run amok, scrambling all existing codes and outdistancing even the most liberal imagination. How to maintain an economy of *tzniut* in a free society is a problem of immense general concern to which religious leaders ought to put their energies. It should not, however, be confused with keeping a woman in her place.

There is, in addition, the fear that there will be a blurring of the sex roles as a woman increasingly does a "man's thing." This again is based on the premise that authority, leadership, initiative, and matters of the spirit (prayer) and the mind (study) are exclusive male prerogatives. (Oddly enough, matters of the spirit and the mind seem somehow feminine; but never mind, we now know that these stereotypes do justice to neither sex.)

To be sure, Judaism places very heavy emphasis on separation. We are always separating things into their categories, spaces, time slots, and so forth: Sabbath from weekday, milk from meat, wool from linen, leaven from unleaven, and yes, men from women. In doing so, the uniqueness of each thing or each being is enhanced; a sense of holiness is miraculously established through the commandments of setting apart.

One cannot deny that Judaism has succeeded in generating a healthy sense of sexual identity, and we must be on guard to preserve this. But it cannot be done in ways which keep women suppressed, nor by means of which women are perceived as less holy or more limited. Moreover, the specific repair that Jewish women are suggesting need not—indeed, will not—break up healthy categories of male and female. How do we know this? From what we see all around us. We once had imagined that women as executives and priests and men as househusbands and kindergarten teachers inevitably would become either masculinized, feminized, or neutered in the process. Not so. Nor have women rabbis become sirens or man-like. Somehow, there must be other, perhaps finer, ways to keep human sexuality intact than the broad, sweeping functions we have inherited.

Finally, we must respond to the oft-expressed fear that equality in Judaism will undermine family life. Whether it is their disaffection with family life that drives some women to feminism or the new knowledge that there is an unstigmatized alternative (divorce) to a marriage of unequals or the heavy feminist emphasis on self-actualization that somehow generates an impatience with the difficulties of building a relationship, the fact is that an exceedingly high proportion of women with feminist leanings have been or are now being divorced. A Jew committed to the idea of family stability is rightly scared.

Yet we must take the issue apart. Every splintered marriage cannot be laid at the doorstep of the women's movement; the attempt to repair circumstances of abuse or powerlessness in a marriage should not be lumped together with, say, a predisposition to creating a tunnel vision about the female self. The shortfalls of women's liberation are used too easily as a cover for maintaining the status quo in Orthodoxy. A healthy family life and feminist values certainly are not mutually exclusive. Similarly, full status for women in the religious life of the community need not of necessity compete with marital bliss. On the contrary, it can enhance the relationship in many subtle ways.

For a marriage to succeed today, there must be a general equation of partners. There may not be perfect equality at every given moment; in fact, there may be large periods of unevenness. One character and personality may dominate; sometimes one partner needs and takes much more than the other. In a good marriage, however, there must be a basic minimum perception of each other as equals. It is to this center that the relationship returns after the inevitable rough spots; it is this cognitive equality that lends stability to marriage.

Such a psychological valence of equals is not generated currently by Halakhah, neither in its assignment of primary mitzvot to men nor in the legal asymmetry of the marriage relationship, as divorce law retrospectively defines it. Those who persist in interpreting Halakhah along the lines of male-female hierarchy truly miss a great leadership opportunity; if only they would use their positions of authority to strengthen a cognitive equality, without which contemporary marriages seem doomed to failure.

On a practical level, extending religious obligations and rights to women does not preclude a healthy family life. Just because a Torah scholar opens up her mind does not mean that she must shut up her womb. Women will not abandon their babies wholesale in order to attend the morning minyan. Those few women who will choose the rabbinate, with its open-ended demands, it is hoped will choose and be chosen by husbands willing to take up the family slack (as countless rebbetzins have done all these years). And a woman who learns how to say kiddush or havdalah or read the Torah with correct cantillations is not destroying the fabric of family life unless we willfully define it that way. The truth is that the rigors of law school or a nine-to-five job or a demanding career represent far greater intrusions into family life than the religious responsibilities that will fall to a woman under a true equality in Judaism. If anything, the participation of women will strengthen ritual and religious institutions, which are themselves major support systems of family life.

These are times for learning new combinations. A young woman, an only child, wanted to say kaddish for her beloved late father. (Kaddish, the daily prayer by mourners during the eleven months following the death of an immediate relative, can be recited only in the presence of a quorum of ten.) It didn't matter to her whether she was counted in the minyan (she wasn't); all she wanted was to recite the ancient memorial prayer, at the appropriate time, in the appropriate setting—in this instance, at the early morning synagogue service. But she had a two-year-old daughter. Her husband, a sociology professor, found it perfectly natural to take full responsibility for the early-morning parenting. When queried by a suspicious friend as to his own liturgical responsibilities, the young father responded with candor: yes, at first it did interrupt his own prayer, but quickly he learned to adjust the schedule to his little daughter's needs, at no loss to his own morning-prayer routine.

I do not want to sound glib on this issue. Family stability is a variable that the community must monitor continually and carefully with each new change. I know that even as we appropriate feminist values to enhance the position of women in Judaism, we must take care to maintain a dialectical stance. Without yielding its legitimate claims to justice and quality, we have to be able to separate ourselves from those elements that can be destructive of Jewish family values: an excessive emphasis on self-actualization that can erode human relationships, a commitment to family, and the need for continuity in a community. But we also must refrain from using family stability as a blanket slogan in the name of which women will continue to be read out of the fullness of the tradition.

What I envision, then, when the theory of Jewish feminism is carried to its practical conclusion, is an adaptation of tradition that will allow for the maturation of woman as Jew—learned, responsible, observant of Halakhah, able to exercise her fullest potential—a woman so committed to the Jewish people that she will incorporate its values and needs as she begins to make the personal choices society now holds out to her.

NOTES

1. See Joseph B. Soloveitchik, "The Lonely Man of Faith," *Tradition* 7 (Summer 1965): 5–67. Rabbi Soloveitchik writes of the "democratization of the God-man confrontation" to all men; it seems that the author also is describing the condition of women.

2. See Leonard Swidler, *Women in Judaism* (Metuchen, N.J.: The Scarecrow Press, 1976).

3. Simone de Beauvoir, *The Second Sex* (New York: Bantam Books, 1953); Rosemary R. Ruether, ed., *Religion and Sexism* (New York: Simon and Schuster, 1974); Michelle Z. Rosaldo and Louise Lamphere, eds., *Women, Culture, and Society* (Palo Alto: Stanford University Press, 1974).

4. Regarding the elimination of conflicting responsibilities, see *Sefer Abudraham ha-shalem* (Jerusalem: Usha, 1959), Order of the Weekday Prayers, the Morning Blessings.

5. Moshe Meiselman, *Jewish Women and Jewish Law* (New York: Ktav, 1978), chap. 16.

6. See, for example, the commentaries on *ve-haya ekev tishma'un,* Deut. 7:12; *naval bi-reshut ha-Torah,* Lev. 12:2, particularly Nachmanides' comments; *shiluah ha-kan,* Deut. 22:6, and commentaries.

7. These are the examples found in the Sifre on Deut. 13:1, explicating the law neither to add to nor subtract from the mitzvot in the Torah. On this verse see also the comments of B. H. Epstein, ed., *Torah temimah* (Jerusalem: Hotza'at Sefer, 1970).

Jewish Women: Coming of Age

THE role of the Jewish woman today is defined by ancient and deeply rooted historical precedents. It is for this reason that contemporary social forces have a different impact upon her role and status than such forces do upon women in general. I shall attempt here to clarify some patterns in the development of women's role in Jewish culture and society. These patterns can serve as a guide to those who feel a need for a change but believe that change should be directed by models within Jewish tradition and should be articulated in proper halakhic categories.

It is difficult to generalize about the condition of Jewish women throughout history, considering the different societies, life-styles, and enormous range of circumstances to which they adapted themselves. Adding to the confusion is the disparity between laws pertaining to women and the historical reality reflected in the same tradition. It is no surprise, then, that this amorphous mass of data has given rise to contradictory positions. At one extreme, some maintain that the Jewish woman was little more than a man's chattel. One source they cite is the commandment from the decalogue: "You shall not covet your neighbor's wife, or his male or female slave, or his ox or his ass, or anything that is your neighbor's" (Exod. 20:14). At the other extreme are those who contend that Judaism placed women on a pedestal—not only was the Jewish woman better off than her sisters in surrounding cultures, but she was also a higher spiritual being than man.

One favorite proof text offered in support of the latter view is the biblical account of creation: woman was created after man, farther up on the ontological scale and therefore the highest form of creation;[1] woman's creation from man's rib is conveniently overlooked. There are also a variety of statements from rabbinic texts to show how the Jewish woman has never stepped down from her pedestal. Since neither of these views obviously reflects the whole truth, we must forgo the luxury of easy generalizations and instead examine as carefully as we can whatever evidence is available.

I

The Bible states that woman was created to serve as a "fitting help-mate for man" (Gen. 2:18). Her chief function was to bear children; failure to do so was a trauma. From the biblical stories of Rachel and Hannah we learn that the barren woman was ridiculed as well as pitied. Worse, in her own eyes she had failed (Gen. 30:1 ff.; 1 Sam. 1:5 ff.). Unmarried, a girl was subject to the authority of her father; only he could release her from vows (Num. 30:4–6). Her father could give her hand in marriage (Gen. 29:16–28; Josh. 15:16; Exod. 21:7; Deut. 22:16). When she married, authority over her was transferred from father to husband (Num. 30:7–16). Her husband was now her master (Gen. 3:16). It is no accident that the Hebrew word *ba'al* means both "husband" and "master."

There are many legal distinctions between men and women drawn from biblical literature: a wife could not initiate divorce, but her husband could divorce her if he found some fault (Deut. 24:1–4). A woman could not give legal testimony or serve as a judge (Deut. 1:13). Inheritance privileges were denied her; indeed, in certain instances, the widow was regarded as part of her husband's property.[2] Daughters, however, could inherit directly from a deceased father, but only if there were no male heirs (Num. 27).

Women were also protected from certain abuses of the law. Although a man paid a *mohar* (bride's price) for his wife, he was not permitted to "resell" her or dispose of her at will, as he could with his other possessions; this applies even to a wife acquired as a captive of war (Deut. 21:14). Furthermore, a Hebrew man was forbidden to sell or force his daughter into prostitution, a wide-spread practice in many parallel ancient cultures.[3] Many biblical narratives, such as the stories of Dinah and Tamar, indicate that a woman's honor was highly guarded, carefully protected, and occasionally avenged (Gen. 34, 38). The rape laws of the Bible are unusual. If a virgin was raped, the rapist was forced to marry her (Deut. 22:28–29). Of course, she was not bound to accept the rapist for a husband, though she might choose to do so, fearing that once she had been violated no one else would have her.[4] In torts and damages, a woman was protected equally under the law, with few exceptions.[5] Finally, the position of a mother was almost sacrosanct: dishonoring a mother warranted the curse of God; cursing a mother was a sin punishable by death (Deut. 27:16; Lev. 20:9).

There is a striking contrast between biblical law and biblical narrative, however. The law presupposes a passive woman whose destiny was controlled by men, but the narrative portrays matriarchs as powerful figures. The text does not stint in its description of women's assertiveness and manipulative powers (Rebekah, Jael, Bathsheba) or the independence and sheer force of their personalities (Rachel, Hannah). There were women prophets and leaders (Miriam, Deborah, Huldah). There were widows of very substantial means, heirs to their husbands' wealthy estates (Judith of Bethulia). Still, here too we must add a qualification: throughout the Bible we find various negative statements about women; although these have no legal weight, they tend to offset somewhat the positive value judgments and narratives.[6]

Beyond the legal and narrative descriptions, there was a profound religious dimension to the biblical woman's life. What were her religious obligations? She was present at Sinai and experienced Revelation. She was obligated to observe numerous positive commandments, such as the dietary laws, the Sabbath, and the hearing of the law every seventh year.[7] Most of the negative commandments were binding upon her. Only males were required to make the three annual pilgrimages to Jerusalem each year (Exod. 23:17, 34:23; Deut. 16:16), yet wives often accompanied their husbands to the Temple, where special areas were set aside for women (1 Sam. 1–2).[8] From biblical times on, the woman figured most importantly in the transmission of religious identity: a Jew is one born to a Jewish mother, regardless of the father's religion.

What emerges is a picture of a woman who was not truly equal but by no means persecuted. Although she suffered limited rights in matrimony, divorce, the courts, and inheritance, she was fairly well protected in most areas under the law and on occasion was able even to rise to a position of national importance. Finally, she had significant religious obligations, albeit fewer than men, to fulfill as a participating member of the community.

One caveat: despite the fond belief of some apologists that the Israelite woman was always better off than her non-Jewish counterpart, ethnographers believe otherwise. Egyptian women were equal to men in the courts; Babylonian women could acquire property, take legal action, make contracts, and share directly in their husbands' inheritance. In most areas, however, the laws regarding women in neighboring cultures were quite similar. The patriarchal marriage customs, for example, are almost identical to the marriage rites described in the Hammurabi codes, circa 1700 B.C.E.[9]

II

The picture of women in talmudic times can also be said to elude easy generalization. All the laws concerning women were discussed in great detail; in some cases her rights were expanded, in others they were limited.

In many areas, women's status was improved under rabbinic law. For example, biblical law suggests that a father could marry off his daughter as he saw fit. The rabbis ruled that a woman should not be given in marriage without her consent (Kiddushin 2b, 44a; Yevamot 19b).[10] The conditions of direct inheritance by daughters were expanded (Bava Batra 9:1; Ketubbot 4:6, 13:3), although a wife still was denied direct inheritance from her husband (Bava Batra 8:1, 109b, 111b; Bava Kamma 42b; Ketubbot 83b). The Talmud ensured a woman's right to retain separate property that she owned prior to marriage (Ketubbot 78a). Furthermore, the biblical *mohar* and the talmudic *nedunyah* (dowry money specified in the marriage contract) were held in escrow, along with any other properties she brought with her into the marriage; all these conditions were stipulated in the ketubah (marriage contract). All of this was returned to her in the event of divorce or the death of her husband (Ketubbot 82b).[11]

The ketubah gave her security and provided a safeguard for many of the woman's rights. Her husband was obligated legally to honor, support, and maintain her in proper style, pay her medical and dental bills, ransom her if she were taken captive, and provide her with a proper burial (Ketubbot 4:4, 51a).[12] The ketubah also protected her in the event of a divorce. Biblical law stated that the husband could divorce his wife if he found something displeasing (*ervat davar*). By obligating the husband to pay his wife a clearly stipulated amount upon divorce—over and above the *mohar* and *nedunyah*—the ketubah tended to discourage hasty decisions. The rabbis provided the woman with additional protection by limiting the legal circumstances under which a man could divorce his wife (Gittin 90a); this did not necessarily improve the status of women, however. Although divorces were less prevalent in talmudic times, it was much harder for a divorced woman to remarry. When a husband had to give valid reasons for divorcing his wife, the result was to attach a certain stigma to her. In the Talmud it was considered disgraceful to marry a divorced woman (Gittin 90b).

Even with the safeguards provided by rabbinic law, the woman was still passive in the creation and dissolution of a marriage. As long as the married woman remained in a position of dependency, her rights generally were ensured; as soon as she tried to assert some mastery over her own life, the doors began to close; "a woman buys herself [her independence and freedom] with a get" (Kiddushin 13b). If the wife wanted a divorce and her husband did not, he could refuse to issue a get.[13] The Talmud gives specific conditions under which a woman could seek a divorce (say, if her husband did not support her in proper style or did not satisfy her sexually) (Ketubbot 5:6, 77a).[14] All of this was an important step in recognizing the woman's prerogative in family law. Rabbinic law, however, allowed no provision for a woman to write and deliver a get or deposit it with a rabbinic court.

Throughout the centuries, rabbis have forced recalcitrant husbands to grant divorces, leveling various sanctions against them when necessary (Arakhin 5:6). Yet the inequity of the divorce law at times has caused extensive delays, humiliations, and extortions.

Arising from this divorce law is the tragic case of the agunah (literally, one who is anchored). An agunah is a woman whose husband has deserted her or is insane, missing, or presumed dead, though death has not been verified by a witness. Since only the husband may write a bill of divorce and under these circumstances none is forthcoming, the woman is not permitted to remarry. Sensitive to the plight of the agunah, rabbinic law made admissible the wife's own testimony concerning her husband's death (Yevamot 93b, 114b–116a); this was done to spare the woman from being anchored to an absentee husband for the rest of her life.

A special law pertained to family violence. A man was forbidden to strike his wife; if he struck her, he had to pay reparations for damages, pain, and shame (Bava Kamma 8:1).[15] Nor could a man aggravate his wife, for her tears will open the gates of heaven and his evil deeds will be known (Bava Metzia 59a). Talmudic law spelled out every facet of the law as it applied to the woman. She was exempt from those positive commandments that must be performed at specific times, such as wearing the tzitzit and tefillin, reciting the *Shema*, and the three complete daily prayer services (Kiddushin 29a; Eruvin 96b; Berakhot 20a–b; Menahot 43a). She was exempt also from certain commandments that were not time-specific (Eruvin 96b).[16] In various communal or group events, she could be a participant-observer but had no equal status in performance of ritual. This held true for the mitzvah of sukkah, the celebration of Simhat Bet ha-Sho'evah, the redemption of the first-born, inclusion in the minyan for grace after meals, and reading the Torah at the communal prayer service (Sukkah 2:18, 53a; Kiddushin 34a; Megillah 47b, 23a). There are important early precedents in Jewish law for women's obligatory participation in liturgical and ritual areas, such as reading the Book of Esther on Purim and lighting the Hanukkah candles (Megillah 4a; Shabbat 23a). Even the denial of the privilege of being called up to the Torah is set forth in language that suggests a positive precedent: women could be (and presumably were) called to the Torah, but the practice was discarded because of the honor of the community (Megillah 23a).[17] Although Halakhah allowed for a female shohet, the community rarely permitted it (Hullin 2a). A woman was obligated by biblical law to say grace, but the Talmud states that a man whose wife (or son) says the blessings for him may be "cursed" in the eyes of the community (Berakhot 20b).[18] Women were separated from men in the Temple (it is not known whether this originated in talmudic or pretalmudic times) because the presence of women could lead to an atmosphere of frivolity (Middot 2:5; Sukkah 5:1–4, 51b).[19] By extension, men and women also were separated in houses of worship.

The Talmud also contains varying judgments about women, which generally reflect the feeling of the individual rabbis who expressed them rather than any particular consensus.[20] There are statements of hostility and disdain, equating women with evil and temptation. "A woman is a pitcher full of filth, yet all run after her" (Shabbat 152a). "Women are greedy, eavesdroppers, lazy, and envious" (Nedarim 31b). More typical are the positive statements of love, affection, and admiration for women—particularly women as wives—and even acknowledgments of dependency upon her: "He shall love her as himself and honor her even more than himself" (Yevamot 62b); "If your wife is small, bend down and whisper in her ear" (Bava Metzia 59a), that is, take counsel with her in all matters.

This attitude of respect, despite the limitations in her legal status, may have been won in the home, the domain in which woman excelled: "What blessing dwells in the home comes from the wife" (Bava Metzia 59a). Her primary, preferred, almost singular role in the home went hand in hand with release from wider social and religious obligations and rights. How perceptive the rabbis were in understanding (or establishing) this connection can be seen in their repeated choice of the psalmist's phrase, "All glorious is the king's daughter within the palace" (Ps. 45:14), which the rabbis interpret as, "The honor of a woman is in her home." They applied this phrase, almost as a talmudic principle, to numerous decisions concerning women (Shevuot 30a). The Talmud seems to have required women to be passive and dependent;[21] many of the laws designed to protect the woman reflect that very passivity. The Talmud extols virtues such as modesty, submission, and forbearance, all qualities that befit a woman who knows her place and stays in it.

True, there were some few exceptional women who rose to intellectual heights or great levels of piety and received recognition for their achievement, but they did not generally participate in the academies of learning or assume leadership positions within the religious community. They were not completely unrecognized, however, for some of their halakhic interpretations and pious acts are recorded in the Talmud and rabbinic literature (Eruvin 63a; Ketubbot 62b–63a).[22]

Even with numerous improvements over their prerabbinic status, women still faced legal and social disabilities. Rabbis made the decisions that defined women's status, role, and obligations. Rabbinic legislation generally supported sharp role distinctions, which tended to favor men. Several decisions placed women in the same category as minors and slaves, the principal difference being that the latter two could grow up and out of their ascribed limitations (Bava Kamma 88a; Berakhot 47b). It was not without good reason that every morning a male Jew would recite the benediction, "Blessed be God . . . for not having created me a woman . . . a slave . . . a gentile." No one for a moment challenged the appropriateness of those daily morning blessings.[23]

III

The Middle Ages reflected the persistence of certain basic inequalities. Still, woman's position gradually improved. In approximately 1025 C.E., Rabbenu Gershom of Mainz, Germany, temporarily banned polygamy upon pain of excommunication (*Shulhan Arukh*, Even ha-Ezer 1:9–11); although its time limit expired in the Hebrew year 5000, polygamy never again was practiced by Jews in Ashkenazic Europe.[24] In oriental countries, where multiple wives were common, Jews continued to practice polygamy right through the modern period.[25] Rabbenu Gershom also formally banned forcible divorce (issuing a get without the wife's consent).[26] Other safeguards against forced divorce also were added, indicating an attempt to ameliorate the situation of women.

Medieval rabbis worked to ease further the plight of the agunah. Every possible decision was made in her favor.[27] If a husband was about to leave the jurisdiction of the court, he was placed under oath not to desert his wife; where his behavior warranted it, he was compelled to divorce his wife before leaving (*Shulhan Arukh*, Even ha-Ezer 154:8–9). In certain instances, a married man could not leave a community without the approval of its leaders, and even then only for a limited period of time and with prearranged guarantees for his family's support.[28] This worked fairly well in a closely knit, interdependent, and religiously observant society. But there still were many instances in which women remained agunot for extended periods of time.

In this century, a Geniza discovery was made of several ketubot more than a thousand years old. In some of them, the wife stipulates that her husband must grant her a divorce if he takes a concubine.[29] It is clear from these documents, which constitute interesting precedents, that some women negotiated their own conditions for a marriage contract.

Inheritance laws relating to the Jewish woman also were upgraded, and many Jewish communities enacted legislation whereby a wife could inherit directly from her husband's estate. As Ze'ev Falk explains, "The widow was made heir by will, though not by law, to part of her husband's estate."[30]

In some exceptional instances, women were allowed to participate in ritual and liturgical areas that formerly were closed to them, such as being counted in a minyan for grace after meals or wearing the ritual garments assigned to men.[31] By the thirteenth century, one scholar was sufficiently self-conscious about the morning benediction "Blessed be God . . . for not having created me a woman" to stress that it was "not because women were inherently inferior."[32] A century later, a parallel prayer for women was inserted into the liturgy: "Blessed be God . . . for having created me according to his will."[33]

Some cite Jewish mysticism of the medieval period as a wedge in the male-oriented structure of Judaism. The kabbalist literature does contain some elements of a feminine theology; the Shekinah, the divine presence, is described in feminine terms. Mysticism, however, had little bearing on the real status of women under Jewish law. Hasidism undermined somewhat the image of the male-dominated house of study as the central locus of Judaism, but the bulk of Jewish tales involving women still centered around the home and family. Only one woman, Hannah Rachel, the Maid of Ludomir, rose to great heights in Hasidic hierarchy. She became a rebbe, leader of a Hasidic sect, and held court behind a curtain.[34]

Women were assiduous in their piety during the medieval period. The laws of niddah (ritual purity and immersion) were observed meticulously. Women themselves increased the severity of the existing laws in this area; this precedent existed in talmudic times as well (Berakhot 31a; Niddah 66a).

Although women were knowledgeable in Jewish observance, Jewish jurisprudence and its history were relatively unknown to them. Although many upper-class Jewish women in Spain and Italy received model Renaissance educations, most Jewish women were not routinely educated in Jewish texts.[35] A popular, though somewhat exaggerated, idealization held that the Jewish woman was content to work, tend to all the family's needs, and educate her young children in religious observance in order to enable her husband and sons to learn Torah. At the end of days she would sit on a footstool at her husband's feet in the Garden of Eden. It was an excellent working relationship, and the institution of marriage was enhanced by common goals and these mutually accepted role designations.

Many ethical wills of the medieval period reflect Jewish attitudes toward women. One father, Judah Ibn Tibbon (1120–ca. 1180) of France, writes in his will:

> My son! I command thee to honor thy wife to thine utmost capacity. She is intelligent and modest, a daughter of a distinguished and educated family. She is a good housewife and mother, and no spendthrift. Her tastes are simple, whether in food or dress. Remember her assiduous attendance of thee in thine illness, though she had been brought up in elegance and luxury. Remember how she afterwards reared thy son without man or woman to help her. Were she a hired nurse she would have earned thy esteem and forbearance; how much the more, since she is the wife of thy bosom, the daughter of the great, art thou bound to treat her with consideration and respect. To act otherwise is the way of the contemptible.[36]

IV

From this brief sketch of the position of Jewish women through the span of many centuries, three principles emerge. Laws concerning woman underwent considerable change; her position was not static. In fact, her status generally improved; most of the legislation concerning women—from biblical through talmudic through medieval—upgraded her position. Further, her condition was influenced to some extent (e.g., monogamy, inheritance) by the status of women in the surrounding cultures and societies. Rabbinic scholars were responsive to society and in many instances incorporated external social norms into their own legal system.

These principles seem to hold much promise as guidelines for the present and future. Still, there are two basic problems we must acknowledge: first, the Jewish woman always was subjected to disabilities in certain areas of Jewish law, just as all women have been faced with disabilities throughout history. That these disabilities have been codified in halakhic decisions, however, makes it more difficult to engender change. Second, the role of the Jewish woman usually was assigned to her by men. The rabbis had the sole power to determine her rights and obligations, which were presented to her as faits accomplis. In other words, she was kept ignorant of the processes of development of Jewish law.

The feminist movement generates new expectations; it has its greatest impact on Jewish women in these two areas. Like all women, Jewish women will not accept inequalities so readily, comfortable though the status quo may be after centuries of conditioning. Jewish women will begin to recondition themselves to what ultimately will be a more satisfactory situation. Indeed, we are witnessing an increase of Jewish women, learned and faithful, who want to enlarge their religious and ritual expression of Judaism. At present, these women are capable of the full range of human expression and learning; they are not asking to be led out, they are asking to enter Jewish life more fully. To discourage them in their endeavors is to act contrary to the ethics of Jewish law, the ethics of human dignity.

Similarly, Jewish women now must begin to study the processes of legal interpretation and innovation to enable them to emerge from a position of ignorant dependency to one of knowledgeable self-reliance and authority. Women must apply themselves seriously to the difficult demands of Jewish scholarship; perhaps this is the only route that eventually will lead to lasting Jewish liberation.

Just as women are expanding their role in general society, so too Jewish women can expect to play a creative role in influencing rabbinic decisions for our time, not only in the area of women's halakhic status but in all areas of Jewish life.

Some confront these challenges by saying that nothing can be changed. This is certainly not true of Halakhah, which is a living system, an ongoing process. There have been stringent and lenient trends in Jewish law in every generation. By combining common sense and a sensitivity to contemporary needs with a desire to remain faithful to the Torah, rabbis in every generation succeeded in preserving a love for the tradition and a sense of its continuity.[37] It is important to emphasize this fact, for contemporary resistance to change has wrapped itself in a cloak of biblical authority and rabbinic immutability. Rabbi Yannai, a leading amora, teaches us otherwise:

> If the law had been given in the form of final rulings, the world could not exist (Rashi explains: it is essential that the Torah can be interpreted this way or that way). Moses said, "Master of the universe, tell me which way is the Halakhah." God answered him, "Follow the majority."[38]

That Jewish women are beginning to grapple with the problems is a healthy sign, because halakhic changes never occurred in a vacuum but always in response to real needs. Thus the extent of the change we shall witness will be in direct proportion to the amount of unrest. It will take a lot to recondition both men and women in the Jewish community to these new values. Maybe unrest and rebellion against stereotypes must be considered the greatest merit, and lack of pride and simple obedience the greatest sin. A large part of the responsibility for change lies with Jewish women who must articulate more openly and more clearly their own needs. Current leaders cannot but be influenced by special pleading; this has happened many times in our history.

For the present generation of Jewish women, a clear mandate can be given. In the areas of marriage and divorce, the remaining disabilities should be removed quickly; enough halakhic groundwork has been laid to allow no room for further procrastination. The unequal status of women in the religious courts needs halakhic reinterpretation and repair. There must be a flowering of women's prayer and an encouragement of leadership roles for women in liturgy. And, most important—the means whereby all of these will be wrought—Jewish women must begin to acquire an intensive Jewish education right up through the level of high-quality rabbinic schools, preferably non-sex-differentiated, so that each will hear the interpretation of the law in the presence of the "other," so that they simultaneously grow in understanding of the tradition. Only then will women become part of the learned elite of our community in whose hands is vested the authority, the power, the leadership, and the inspiration.

An eternal Judaism will integrate and grow with such changes because these changes are wholly compatible with the spirit of the fundamental principle of Judaism—that every human being is created in the image of God.[39]

NOTES

1. See Aaron Soloveitchik, "A Jewish View of the Higher Nature of Woman," *The Jewish Horizon*, November 1969.

2. This is one conclusion that can be drawn from the institution of levirate marriage. In certain instances this law worked to the disadvantage of the woman; she was not free to remarry as she pleased. In other instances the law offered her protection: she did not go unredeemed, confined to widowhood and childlessness (Gen. 38). At some point in biblical history the law of levirate marriage became a matter for the clan and not only the immediate family of the deceased (Ruth 2–4). The Bible records the full range of human drama—love, protection, abuse, power—that was played out as a result of the loose connection between a man's wife and his possessions (2 Sam. 16:21–22; 1 Kings 2:22). See also Roland de Vaux, *Ancient Israel: Its Life and Institutions* (New York: McGraw-Hill, 1965), pp. 20–21, 38.

3. It is true that Lot was prepared to give his daughters to the townsmen to have their sexual pleasure, but this was seen only as a drastic measure to save the lives of Lot's household guests (Gen. 19:8).

4. This law, like unjust rape laws throughout most of human history, seems to imply some degree of complicity on the part of the victim. In that time, however, this biblical law protected her. Moreover, it seems clear from the other laws on rape that the woman was considered a victim; there was a very sharp delineation of the circumstances under which she could be considered an accomplice (Deut. 22:13–28).

5. In this respect, biblical law was years ahead of contemporary law, where court settlements and insurance claims paid to women were, until

recently, minuscule compared to those paid to men for similar damages. The Talmud teaches that payments for pain and shame were made directly to the woman but payments for healing and loss of work were made to her husband. Another is the case in which damages for injury to the fetus carried by a pregnant woman are paid to the husband (Exod. 21:22).

6. See Phyllis Bird, "Images of Women in the Old Testament," in *Religion and Sexism*, ed. Rosemary R. Ruether (New York: Simon and Schuster, 1974), pp. 41–88.

7. The wife is not mentioned specifically in the Sabbath law (neither in Exod. 20:10 nor in Deut. 5:14), but daughters and female slaves are. Tradition teaches that the wife is included in the "you" addressed to her husband in the masculine singular. The reference to "gather the people" explicitly states "men and women" (Deut. 31:12; Neh. 8:2–3).

8. See Middot 2:5 and Sukkot 51b for fuller descriptions.

9. For a good cross-cultural comparison, see de Vaux, *Ancient Israel*, and Martin Noth, *The Laws in the Pentateuch and Other Studies* (Philadelphia: Fortress Press, 1966).

10. This rabbinic decision is pegged to the story of Rebekah, who is asked for her consent. Here, as in other instances, the *asmakhta* is selective, overlooking evidence that points up the reverse situation: that the marriage was contracted by the "consenting" males—Eliezer representing Abraham on one side and Laban and his father, Betuel, on the other. The finality of that agreement is confirmed by the description of Eliezer prostrating himself in thankfulness to God and then paying the bride's price to the new in-laws; only then do they go off and consult Rebekah. Such is the power of *asmakhta* —to interpret Halakhah and enable it to be continuous with Torah. See the discussion in Chanoch Albeck, ed., *Bereshit Rabbah* (Jerusalem: Wahrmann Books, 1965), vol. 2, 24:57 and p. 653, n. 3.

11. He was entitled, however, to invest her property for profit, which became part of his estate, not hers (Ketubbot 65b). In two cases, in 1958 and 1971, the Supreme Court of Israel reversed the rabbinic court's decision based on Ketubbot 65b and upheld the 1951 equal rights law by abolishing the husband's right to profits from his wife's property. See Stephen Beiner, "Israeli Divorce Law: A Comparative Study" (unpublished), p. 10.

12. Maimonides underscores the historical development of the different protections accorded her. See *Mishneh Torah*, Hilkhot Ishut 12:2.

13. It is only the husband who may write and deliver the get; until the eleventh century, the wife's consent was not even required legally. In practice, however, the absolute right of the husband to put aside his wife was more theoretical than practical. Throughout the discussions of divorce in the Talmud and the responsa, it becomes obvious that this theoretical right had ceased to exist for centuries before Rabbenu Gershom's ban. Even with requirement for consent, there was still resistance to Rabbenu Gershom's formal decree, which was not incorporated into Sephardic tradition until much later. Maimonides reaffirms the original principle that a woman can be divorced with or without her consent (*Mishneh Torah*, Hilkhot Gerushin 1:2). Thus, the importance of an unfolding Halakhah to stabilize gains in women's rights. See *Shulhan Arukh*, Even ha-Ezer 119:6, Isserles commentary; Responsa Asheri 42:1.

14. See also *Shulhan Arukh*, Even ha-Ezer 76:11. Motivated by an awareness of the sexual needs of women as well as men, the Talmud established minimum requirements for the frequency of intercourse, which vary according to the occupation of the husband (Ketubbot 61b–62b).

15. Maimonides seems to be the first to specify husband-wife relationships. See Maimonides, *Mishneh Torah*, Hilkhot Hovel u-Mazzik 4:16–18.

16. See Saul Berman, "The Status of Women in Halakhic Judaism," *Tradition* 14 (Winter 1973): 5–28.

17. One later interpretation (Ritva, Megillah 4a) is that men in the synagogue would be put to shame if a woman was able to read the Torah and recite its blessings while they were not able to do so. See David Feldman, "Woman's Role and Jewish Law," *Conservative Judaism* (Summer 1972): 29–39.

18. Rashi's commentary interprets "cursed" as shamed, similar to the idea of *kevod ha-tzibbur* in a communal setting of Torah reading: a man would be shamed if his wife could say the blessing but he could not.

19. The Mishnah teaches, "Originally *ezrat nashim* (the women's hall) was all level; only later did they surround it with a balcony so that women should look on from above while the men were below them—in order that they not be intermingled." There is no extant gemara on these passages; subsequent commentators, however, all suggest that this was done specifically for the Simhat Bet ha-Sho'eva celebration. It seems that women were initially allocated a special courtyard or hall in the Temple complex. When the men moved the celebration to the women's area, they (priests, Levites, and Israelite men) expropriated the area for their celebration, which was quite spectacular. They constructed a balcony so that women could look on.

20. Judith Hauptman, "Images of Women in the Talmud," in *Religion and Sexism*, ed. Rosemary R. Reuther, pp. 197–208; Leonard Swidler, *Women in Judaism* (Metuchen, N.J.: The Scarecrow Press, 1976), chaps. 4–5.

21. Even the talmudic description of the optimal coital position reflects this attitude (i.e., the husband should be on top because he should take the initiative) because the commandment for procreation is upon him, not upon her, and because she is the receiver, he the giver. See Masekhet Kallah, at the end of Berakhot. In Masekhet Kallah Rabati, this baraita appears at the end of chapter 1. See also *Shulhan Arukh*, Orah Hayyim 240.

22. Swidler, *Women in Judaism*, pp. 97–111.

23. The blessing is attributed to Rabbi Meir (Menahot 43b); it is also found in Tosephta Berakhot 6:23 in a more original form. In both these sources a legal rather than social reason is given: "Blessed be God . . . for not having created me a woman" because woman is not obligated to fulfill the commandments, such as tefillin on his head, tefillin on his arm, tzitzit on his garment—all of which continually remind him of God's presence. The blessing was inserted into the daily morning prayer with no accompanying explanation.

24. This would have been socially unacceptable in a Christian culture, where the celibate life was considered ideal. Oddly enough, six centuries later Rabbi Jacob Emden criticized the original ban as an aping of gentile customs. Emden, *She'elat Ya'avetz* (Lemberg: 1884), 2:15.

25. Simon ben Zemach Duran, *Sefer ha-Tashbetz* (Amsterdam, 1741), no.

94; Rabbi Solomon (son of Duran), *Teshuvot Rashbash*, no. 624; *Teshuvot ha-Rashba* (Vilna: Romm, 1881), vol. 4, no. 257. See also *Teshuvot ha-Rashba* (Vilna: Romm, 1875), vol. 3, no. 446. In 1948, when the Yemenite Jews were brought to Israel in Operation Magic Carpet, many arrived with several wives in tow. In response, the chief rabbis of Israel called a national rabbinic conference in 1950 and passed a takkanah making monogamy binding on all Jews, regardless of their social or geographic origins. Existing polygamous unions were allowed to continue unaffected, however.

26. In European Sephardic culture, where Rabbenu Gershom's ban was not acknowledged, the community stepped in to protect a woman against a forcible divorce. Rabbi Solomon ben Aderet cites an ordinance where consent of the majority of the community was required for divorce.

27. Isak Farkas Kahan, *Sefer ha-agunot* (Jerusalem: Mossad Harav Kuk, 1954), esp. "Release to (re) Marry Granted to a Witness Who Testified on the Death of a Husband," pp. 31ff.

28. Benjamin Ze'ev, *Responsa* (Jerusalem: Stitsberg, 1959), no. 64. See also Kahan, *Sefer ha-agunot*.

29. It is interesting to note that these stipulations were made in ketubbot of oriental origin, where polygamy was neither forbidden nor unknown. S. D. Goitein, "The Position of Women According to the Cairo Geniza Documents," *Papers of the Fourth World Congress of Jewish Studies*, vol. 2 (Jerusalem, 1968), pp. 177–79; idem, "Jewish Women in the Middle Ages," *Hadassah Magazine* (October 1973). See also Mordecai Friedman, "The Ethics of Medieval Jewish Marriage," in *Religion in a Religious Age*, ed. S. D. Goitein (Cambridge, Mass.: Association for Jewish Studies, 1974), pp. 83–101; Ze'ev Falk, *Jewish Matrimonial Law* and *The Divorce Action by the Wife in Jewish Law* (Jerusalem: Hebrew University, 1973).

30. Falk, *Jewish Matrimonial Law*, cites the following: Mordecai, Nashim 70; Meir of Rothenberg, *Responsa* (Prague ed.) 875; Joel Muller, *Teshuvot hakhmei Zarfat ve-Lotir* (Vienna, 1881), pp. 13, 47, 49, 51. On the question of direct inheritance, see Isadore Epstein, ed., *The Responsa of Rabbi Solomon ben Adreth* (New York: Ktav, 1968), p. 85f.

31. Mordecai, Berakhot 173; Piskei Mordecai, Hilkhot K'tanot 949. See *Mishneh Torah*, Hilkhot Tzitzit 3:9; Eruvin 96a; Rosh Hashanah 33a; Hullin 110b, 86b; Hagigah 16b; and the Ran's comments on Rabbenu Tam's ruling of women permitted to say a blessing on positive time-bound commandments in Ran, Commentary on Alfasi (Rosh Hashanah, 955).

32. As mentioned above, n. 23, the "more mitzvot" reason is given in the Talmud and the Tosefta. Rabbi Yaakov Anatoli, a thirteenth-century halakhist, repeats it with his disclaimer about women's inferiority. On this same theme, see Samson Raphael Hirsh, *Commentary on the Torah* (London: I. Levy, 1962), Lev. 23: 43.

33. *Sefer Abudraham ha-shalem* (Jerusalem: Usha, 1959), Order of the Weekday Prayers, Morning Blessings.

34. See Harry M. Rabinowicz, *World of Hasidism* (London: Valentine, Mitchell, 1970), pp. 205–7.

35. A tradition deriving from an interpretation of Rabbi Eliezer's statement, "He who teaches his daughter Torah is as if he has taught her lewdness" (Sotah 3:4). Torah there refers to the possible merit a *sotah* may have

that would warrant postponing punishment. Very few rabbinic statements have been taken so far afield from their context. Nonetheless, one must point to the social and religious values in the Jewish community that permitted interpretations—so negative to women's intellectual capacity—to crop up continually throughout the rabbinic, medieval, and modern periods. See Israel Abrahams, *Jewish Life in the Middle Ages* (New York: Atheneum, 1969), p. 340f; Simcha Assaf, *Sources in the History of Education in Israel* (Tel Aviv: Dvir, 1954), vol. 1.

36. Israel Abrahams, ed., *Hebrew Ethical Wills* (Philadelphia: The Jewish Publication Society of America, 1976), p. 78.

37. Eliezer Berkovits, "Conversion According to Halakhah—What Is It?" *Judaism* 23 (Fall 1974): 467–78; Emanuel Rackman, *One Man's Judaism* (New York: Philosophical Library, 1970).

38. Jerusalem Talmud, Sanhedrin, ch. 4, halakhah 2 (16a).

39. See Irving Greenberg, "Jewish Tradition and Contemporary Problems," in *Relationships between Jewish Tradition and Contemporary Social Issues* (New York: Yeshiva University, 1969).

Women and Liturgy

Scene 1: A Friday evening in Jerusalem, Spring 1975

IT was with a sense of well-being that I made my way to the synagogue, a small intimate place with two hundred seats in the men's section and sixty to seventy in the women's balcony. My husband had left the house fifteen minutes earlier with our three older children; I decided to take the two younger ones, whom I hadn't managed to get ready on time.

I always have felt that the nicest communal prayer occasion is the Sabbath eve service: it "opens" the Sabbath; it's relatively short; and, most special, there is generally more singing than at any other time. Yet, I rarely go to shul on Friday nights, at least I didn't during this stage of my life. First, it's not expected of me. Second, no matter what hour of the day Shabbat starts, there is always the last-minute rush ("erev-Shabbat neurosis," a friend calls it)—a missing button, the Shabbat timer to set, the *blech* (tin covering) on the stove, clean towels for the guests, the silver hallah knife that needs polishing, and inevitably, no matter how hard we try, J.J.'s missing Shabbat slacks, jacket, shoe, or tie (crumpled up in his pocket from last week). So, after I light my candles and kiss everyone out the door, I am usually grateful for a little quiet time.

On this Friday night, however, it felt wonderful to be in shul. Upstairs there were a few women, a dozen or so teenage girls, and a slightly larger group of little girls doing what little girls usually do in shul—saying *Shmoneh Esreh* (the Eighteen Benedictions) with great dispatch and then going about their real business of playing

75

together. I found something very pleasing about the low attendance in the women's section, even though on Shabbat mornings I always appreciate the high attendance in the women's section. Whether it was the contrast to a "full house" or the beautiful communal singing, I felt myself very much a part of the assembled congregation, the *edah*, and, by extension, all of Jerusalem, all of *klal Yisrael*.

At one point I found a few moments to examine the siddur (prayer book) I held. It opened with an introduction to the laws of tefillin: "Every single Jew is required to put on tefillin each weekday." At first I was stunned. How progressive, I thought, to find such a siddur in an Orthodox synagogue! Then I noted the publisher's date: 1905. In 1905 siddur compilers spoke the language of the community: every single Jew, the whole community, the entire spiritual congregation. But—I checked myself—it all refers only to men. Quietly, unselfconsciously, with one stroke of the pen, the complete class of Jewish women simply was excised.

Oddly enough, I felt neither insulted nor shocked nor even emotionally distanced from the rest of the congregation. The compiler of the siddur might not have thought "woman" when he wrote "every single Jew," but I still felt I belonged. For a fleeting moment I experienced only the inner equivalent of looking askance; then I continued with business as usual. My newly raised consciousness was no match for layer upon layer of conditioning. Besides, I said to myself, this was 1975 and things were changing.

Scene 2: Simhat Torah in a large, bustling, modern Orthodox synagogue, 1979

As is not uncommon midway through the hakafah ceremonies, the decorum is beginning to unravel. The synagogue is packed with eight hundred people—men, women, and hundreds of children. Some two hundred men already have completed their ritual circuit around the synagogue with a Torah in their arms. Now they are beginning to get restless; they want to get on with the service. A few have given up and gone home to conclude the prayers alone.

Those men who haven't had their hakafah yet are also a bit impatient. The women chat, give out candy, keep a watchful eye to see when their husbands and sons have a hakafah. In previous years the men returned the Torah to the ark passing through the women's aisles, and the women would stand up to kiss the Torah. But this year the rabbi said no, so the women's section is less sober than usual. The children run around in groups, parading their flags, filling their bags with candy. At one point the noise level reaches a new high. The rabbi pounds on the podium. "Let us have silence here. We won't complete the service until every single person here has had a hakafah." For a fleeting moment I find my husband's eyes across the partition. He smiles. He knows.

Scene 3: The heavenly kingdom, the year 6000, as Jews count time

An American rabbi is called to the final judgment. He comes before the heavenly throne and the angels plead on his behalf. His deeds are many, his sins few. All his life he has been guided by the principles of Torah and by his desire to secure a proper place in the world to come.

A modest, unassuming man, he is shocked when informed that he is guilty of hubris, the sin of exceeding pride. Every Yom Kippur, as he reviewed the litany of sins in relation to his own life, excess pride was low on the list. "Why?" he cries. "What have I done?"

The angels oblige. They flash before him an earthly scene, and then another and another. It is Shabbat on earth. The setting is a women's minyan. The rabbi recognizes many of the women— friends, students, and members of his congregation. The scene shifts to the heavenly throne. The Holy One, blessed be He, is pleased with His children Israel. His name has been invoked; He is called again and again, in a thousand places over all the earth, to hear the pleas and praises of His children.

Suddenly, however, there is a great stirring around the heavenly throne. Something has gone awry. The women have withheld praises that His children in a thousand other places on earth call out with full voice, words and phrases that attest to the holiness and kingship of God.

"My daughters, My daughters, why do you deny My kingship?"

The women reply: "Our brothers, our leaders, have so instructed us."

Scene 4: Shabbat morning, the apartment of David and Phyllis and their three young sons

It is 10:00 A.M. and Phyllis, a school psychologist, is trying to get the boys ready for shul. The oldest boy, Avrum Zev, age five, is still running about in his pajamas. Phyllis admonishes him, "Hurry up, you're making us all late. I'll miss the whole davening by the time we get there."

The immortal words of five-year-old Avrum Zev ring out: "What are you rushing for? Mommies don't have to daven!"

The issue is not what a siddur compiler of 1905 thinks or doesn't think about women, nor is it a simple-minded theology of God wants the heart, nor is it the incredible power of early conditioning. It is, however, a consideration of all these factors as we turn to examine the issue of women and liturgy.

The Situation Today

The phrase "women and liturgy" covers a wide variety of responses. The situation generally can be described as follows: halakhic assignment of partial responsibility for women and a public invisibility matched by even lower rates of private performance. This minimalness cuts across dimensions of time and space; it is to be found in daily prayer as well as in annual holiday liturgies, in family rituals as well as in communal celebrations of rites of passage. It seems that the Jewish women's reflex for liturgy, if it ever was fully exercised, has atrophied.

Let us attempt to trace the pattern in one prototypical area—formal, fixed time, that is, daily prayer. Most Jewish women, all across the religious spectrum, hardly open a prayer book from one Shabbat to the next, if that often.[1] The contrast to Jewish men is particularly striking in the Orthodox community, where the discipline of daily prayer is observed almost universally. To what extent does this gap between men and women reflect Halakhah? Hardly at all. In fact, almost perversely it would seem, women have assumed precisely those liturgical responsibilities from which they were exempt—the additional Sabbath and holiday prayers—and by and large have neglected those parts of the liturgy that were required halakhically of them—the daily *shaharit* and *minhah* prayers.[2] To extend the point further: women are obligated in *tefilat sheva* (the Sabbath equivalent of *Shmoneh Esreh*) and in hearing the response of the Torah on Shabbat. Yet, most women's sections tend to fill up only toward the very end of the Torah reading.

How did all this come to be? Did Orthodox Jewish women simply decide, arbitrarily and en masse, to resign from day-to-day liturgical responsibility? I think not, given the general faithfulness to Halakhah with which they comport themselves. Nor is one isolated factor sufficient to explain the situation. Rather, the answer lies in a complex set of variables, all somehow interrelated: the unfolding of the law through history, the domino effect of laws that exempt upon laws that bind, the self-image of women that grows out of wider halakhic and historical factors, and the psychic impact of communal unaccountability upon private performance.

The Halakhah

The mitzvah of prayer is derived from the biblical verse, "to love the Lord your God and to serve Him with all your heart and with all your soul" (Deut. 11:13). The Talmud defines "service of the heart" as prayer and proceeds to give it shape and form (Taanit 2a; Arakhin 11a). The tannaim, the early masters of talmudic law, also teach us that women have fewer liturgical responsibilities: for example, "Women are exempt from reciting the *Shema* and wearing tefillin, but are obligated in *tefilah* (prayer), mezuzah, and grace after meals" (Berakhot 3:3). (Although there is an enormous range of responses that come under the rubric of *tefilah*, in rabbinic language it generally refers to the daily *Shmoneh Esreh* of *shaharit* and *minhah*.)

The amoraim, the later masters who studied that particular mishnaic text, had difficulty with the *tefilah* obligation for women. Did not the tannaim, they asked (Kiddushin 1:7), also teach the general principle that women, unlike men, are exempt from all positive commandments that must be performed within a fixed time frame? Why then should women be obligated, in *tefilah*, that is, specific prayers that can be recited only within the appropriate time slots?

The amoraim answered their own question somewhat ambiguously: "Women are obligated in prayer because prayer is a plea for mercy, and women, too, need mercy. One may think, however, that *tefilah* is a fixed-time positive commandment (with women exempt), for Scripture states: 'Evening and morning and afternoon I will pray incessantly' (Ps. 55:18). Therefore, the Mishnah explicitly informs us that women are obligated" (Berakhot 20a).

There are two ways of understanding this pericope:

1. *Tefilah* indeed falls into the category of fixed-time prayer, from which women ordinarily would be exempt. But because of its unique functions—a plea for mercy—the exemption is overridden, and women consequently are obligated. This view is held by Rashi, the Tosafists, Nahmanides, and the majority of later halakhists.
2. Despite what we may think otherwise, prayer, like mezuzah and grace after meals, is a positive commandment *not* limited to time. Therefore the Mishnah comes to teach us that women are obligated. This latter interpretation is held by Maimonides and his disciples (*Mishneh Torah*, Hilkhot Tefilah 1:1–3).[3] He bases it on the fact that the obligation for *tefilah* originally comes from the Torah. Since no set times are given in the Torah (but rather were formulated subsequently by the rabbis), the basic and original commandment cannot be considered time-limited, so women are obligated.

Maimonides spells out the Torah requirements for *tefilah*, and they are indeed rather informal: daily prayer, beginning with praise of God, followed by plea and request, and closing with praise and gratitude. Each person can fashion it according to his own ability. In discussing rabbinic *tefilah*—fixed time, fixed text—Maimonides does not say women were exempt; neither does he say they were obligated. Thus, the distinction between formal-text, fixed-time prayer for men and spontaneous prayer for women was established.

As with many details of tradition, the laws of women and daily liturgy took several turns through history. For example, the sixteenth-century *Shulhan Arukh* generally followed the Maimonidean view of things, and this issue was no exception: "Even though women are exempt from reciting the *Shema* they nevertheless are obligated in *tefilah*, for *tefilah* is a positive commandment which is not limited to time " (*Shulhan Arukh*, Orah Hayyim, Hilkhot Tefilah 106:2). On the other hand, the *Shulhan Arukh* does not identify the exact nature of the requirements for women's *tefilah*, nor does it cite the informal categories that Maimonides offered. Moreover, the entire section of the *Shulhan Arukh* in which the above law is found quite clearly refers to the formal, fixed-time prayers.

One century later, the law took another turn, as an influential halakhist comments on the above passage in the *Shulhan Arukh:*

> The law here is similar to Maimonides, who was of the opinion that the commandment of *tefilah* is from the Torah. . . . The Torah requirement [for *tefilah*] is once a day, in any form one desires. Therefore, the majority of women do not pray with any sort of regularity, for they seem to fulfill their obligations by reciting some sort of plea in the morning immediately after saying the blessing over washing the hands. According to the Torah obligation, that is sufficient to fulfill the mitzvah. Perhaps the Rabbis of the Talmud really never required of them any more than that [in the passage "Women are . . . obligated in *tefilah*, mezuzah, and grace" (Berakhot 3:3)]. But Nachmanides and most other poskim view *tefilah* as a rabbinic commandment [with formal, fixed-time prayers, with women nevertheless obligated].[4]

Here we see the interweaving of halakhic tradition, sociology, and ex post facto positioning all in one brief commentary.

At the turn of the twentieth century, the two most authoritative *poskim* point out the discrepancy between the majority halakhic view and common practice:

Tefilah is of rabbinic origin and refers to the *Shmoneh Esreh* compiled by the Men of the Great Assembly. Even though technically women should be exempt [for it is time-fixed], they are nonetheless obligated to say *Shmoneh Esreh* of *shaharit* and *minhah*. . . . And they should be admonished to recite the *Shmoneh Esreh* . . . and the *Shema*."[5]

Perforce, we must consider that our women are not careful in fulfilling all three daily *tefilot*.[6]

To sum up: what seems originally to have been an obligation for women largely has lost its binding force. One contributing factor is the minority view that legitimated a less rigorous discipline for women. But there are many other factors, not the least of which is the general exemption of women from certain mitzvot.

The Exemption

The basic principle seems clear enough. Any commandment that one must perform actively within a given time limit (hereafter referred to as a time imperative) is not binding upon women. A time imperative means that if you haven't performed the action during the proper time allotted for it, you cannot go back and make it up out of its time slot (Kiddushin 1:7). For example, if a man wears tzitzit at night he has not fulfilled the biblical commandment of wearing tzitzit, for tzitzit must be worn by day. Other examples of time imperatives: dwelling in the sukkah and blessing the lulav (required during the holiday of Sukkot), donning tefillin (to be done by day) (Tosephta Kiddushin 1:10). The notion of fixed time is rather elastic, ranging from one segment of one special day to the entire period of daylight every day of the year.

From the exemption of women from tefillin the rabbis derive several other exemptions: counting the omer, hearing the shofar, and reciting the *Shema*. That women are not considered part of the minyan also is derived rabbinically from the laws of women and tefillin.

From our twentieth-century perspective we are compelled to ask, "Why should the rabbis have interpreted tradition as exempting women in the first place?" Interestingly, we find no specific rationale in the Talmud. Either the reason was so obvious that it did not warrant discussion, or it was discussed but not recorded. Some would argue that each specific detail was given to Moses at Sinai. In any event, what emerges is exemption by gender rather than by function, a standard called into question by contemporary notions of sexual equality.

Although the Talmud offers no rationale, it does present a most usable insight into the arbitrary nature of the exemption principle. When challenged as to the inappropriateness of applying the principle to certain mitzvot, Rabbi Yohanan replied, "Even though the Mishnah already has stated several exceptions to the principle, that list was not exhaustive. Other exceptions have been or could be added" (Kiddushin 34a). To paraphrase, the principle is not necessarily consistent. For those so inclined to interpret it that way, Rabbi Yohanan's statement opens the door to historical emendation of particulars that flow in or out of the principle—which is, in fact, what has happened.[7]

Subsequent scholars nevertheless did try to attach some meaning to the exemption. Their varied explanations shed light on the social attitudes toward women in a given era; and, as we shall see, the negative or positive valence toward women is not a linear progression.

1. The sex-hierarchy theory, with men in the advantaged position (fourteenth century).

Women were exempt from time imperatives because a woman is subservient to her husband and should be free to tend to his needs as they arise. So as to eliminate possible time conflicts between serving God and serving her husband, and in order to foster harmony in the home, God exempts women from certain of His commandments that had to be performed at a specific time.[8]

2. The sex-hierarchy theory, with women assigned the advantage, as in Samuel Raphael Hirsch's view of the moral and spiritual superiority of women (nineteenth century).

Freeing women from certain fixed-time commandments most certainly can not be on account of their being considered in any way less worthy or important. . . . But more likely, the Torah did not impose these mitzvot on women because it did not deem women in need of these mitzvot. By means of symbolic procedures, these fixed-time commandments serve to spur us on afresh from time to time. The Torah allows that women have a special love and great fervor in serving God through their unique calling in life [the family role]. Moreover, in that calling, they are less in danger of the temptations that men face in business and professional life. . . . In all the sins into which our nation has sunk, it has been the merit of the righteous women that has preserved us.[9]

3. Lack of mental control (thirteenth century). A midrash explains why women are included in the exemption along with children and slaves: "Because of the single-minded nature of all three; a child has foolishness on his mind, and a slave is slavishly bound up with his master" (Yalkut Shimoni, 1 Sam. 1:13).[10] This theory differs from the first insofar as that one is a functional exemption (serving her husband); here, a broader, more pervasive value judgment of the female personality is made.

4. The time-control theory in reverse (twentieth century). Because of their menses, their own biological clocks, women are more sensitive to the passage of time than men are. Women therefore do not need certain mitzvot that mark time. Men, however, do need such mitzvot to help them become more aware of the cosmic dimension of time. This view has been offered by a number of contemporary rabbis.

5. Exemption as a function of the private and public nature of a particular ritual (twentieth century). This theory, propounded by Saul Berman, seems the most sophisticated, relevant, and fresh analysis of the principle of exemption. Berman points out that time is a weak correlative factor, with more exceptions to the rule than otherwise. He then ferrets out a more consistent, uniform factor to explain why an item is in or out of the exemption—the public or private performance of a mitzvah. Because Jewish society dictated that women function primarily as "inside" persons, the rabbis did whatever was in their interpretive power to prevent women from being summoned into the public sector.[11] Berman's theory neatly explains women's lack of status in the minyan, women not permitted to be called to the Torah, women disqualified as witnesses in Jewish courts of law—all of which would take women into the public sector.

This theory is significant because it not only sheds light on the principle but also on the input of sociology into halakhic creativity. The rabbis interpreted tradition in light of the expectation and social understanding of men and women of their times. I shall return to this point later.

Although both positive and negative reasons have been advanced, it seems that the principle and practice of exemption generally yielded negative self-images of women regarding a discipline of steady prayer. What tilts the balance perhaps is the language of the principle itself: "Women, slaves, and children are exempt" (Kiddushin 1:7). Of course, women are not equated with slaves or to children, but the phrase subtly suggests that, in the eyes of the Halakhah, women shared with slaves and children a status lower than the adult free male. Not lost on women, surely, was the realization that individual slaves and male children could grow up or out of these ascribed categories, but the entire class of women forever retained a status of "exempt," "released," "unaccountable."

Thus the impact of laws that exempt upon laws that bind was far-reaching. The exemptions not only weakened women's commitment to prayer but also repressed any desire to be formally considered equal members of the holy community.

The Public/Private Affair

Communal prayer differs from private prayer in several respects. It needs a quorum of ten (Megillah 23b); it is a more desirable form of prayer (Berakhot 6a, 8a); certain passages, generally known as the *davar she-bi-kedushah* (holiness) passages, may be recited only in a quorum (Megillah 5b).[12]

The minyan is a relationship of halakhic interdependence, an unspoken yet powerful symbol of human interdependence, of what community is all about. Each person in a minyan enables every other person to fulfill the requirements of a minyan. Conversely, one who is not obligated in the mitzvah of *tefilah be-tzibbur* (prayer in a quorum) cannot enable another to fulfill the obligation.

Prayer in a minyan, then, is preferable to private prayer; it strengthens a sense of kinship. In traditional Judaism, however, women may neither constitute a minyan nor enable others to constitute one.[13] A certain legal symmetry is apparent: just as women are released from the responsibilities of public prayer, so they are "relieved" of the rights of communal prayer. When women do pray, then, it becomes a function of intermittent and tardy synagogue attendance, an experience that is muted further by the fact that women are on the periphery—psychic as well as real—of the gathered assembly.

Add this public invisibility to exemption by sex, and the whole situation becomes one that is hardly designed to engender serious prayer—which is why prayer has become in Judaism a male prerogative. Five-year-old Avrum Zev knows it; I suspect his three-year-old brother knows it too. And so do three hundred women.

A few years ago my family and I spent the Passover holidays at a Catskill hotel, where the guests all were Orthodox. On the first night of Passover a strange sight greeted my eyes. Decked around the lobby, perfectly coiffed and attired, were three hundred women, sitting and chatting; their husbands were in the hotel synagogue attending evening services. It was a clear case of conditioning and expectation. None of the women there had any domestic or child-care tasks that compelled their time and attention at the moment, as perhaps might have been the case at home. A look at the women's section in the shul made the picture complete—a torn, raggedy-looking curtain covering the mehitzah, completely blocking vision and blurring sound. There just as well could have been a sign on the back door: WOMEN NEED NOT APPLY.

Another image immediately surfaced: room 204 in the administration building at the Catholic college where I once had taught. The school was founded over a hundred years ago by a female order, and during the decade following Vatican II, it underwent many changes, all of which reflected the liberalizing tendencies of the Church. The nuns "kicked the habit," the school went coed, courses on Judaism were now taught by a Jew instead of a priest, and so on. But some things didn't change. Every single day at 12:30, a group of Catholic women, religious and lay, from the college president to the administrative assistant in the printing room, would meet for a half-hour in an ad-hoc chapel—room 204—to say Mass. Equally impressive to me was to learn that this practice had been going on for one hundred years, with never a day missed. The numbers weren't huge, but it was steady, and it was an available model to the students. Try as I did to search my mind for a parallel group in my own community, I could not. Individuals, yes, but a group of adult women to serve as a model in much the same way that a minyan of men serves as a spiritual and mental model for individual prayer? Not one.

The Power of Conditioning Versus New Realities

It seems the situation calls for repair. But first we must ask: What is really so bad with the way things are? Most women who observe mitzvot have very strong feelings of Jewish commitment, without all that prayer. Most traditional women are very comfortable with the status quo and really are not looking for extra mitzvot. Why speak of others? Let me share my own feelings and mixed emotions.

I always have felt at ease, even pleased, with the notion that men have certain mitzvot and women others. Part training, part conditioning, my own prayer habits are considerably less developed than most males who find themselves at the same point on the denominational continuum. I still have considered myself very fulfilled as a Jew. Moreover, I must profess that I experience feelings of pleasure as I observe men meeting their prayer obligations. This is not simply a surface pleasantness. Rather, the experience touches me at some very deep levels of spiritual and sexual comprehension, the essence of which I am unable to articulate, even to myself.

What is that inner contentment I feel as I watch my husband and sons put on tefillin? How to account for that surge of pride as I observe them reciting the afternoon prayer—at home, or in a quiet spot at the edge of a sandy beach, or even in a Manhattan phone booth as dusk approaches at a faster pace than rush-hour traffic? Why do I have a sense of satisfaction and completion without feeling the least bit motivated to join? Is it that in spite of what I know intellectually, emotionally I have come to think of prayer as a "man's thing," with men alone being so commanded. Had the rabbis interpreted revelation not in light of conventional wisdom but rather with some divine insight into human nature, so that shared liturgical responsibilities in some way ultimately would fail? Could it be that what takes place in a males-only minyan keeps males from searching out less desirable locales for male bonding, such as bars, poolrooms, and men's clubs? Besides, who wants to rise earlier for prayer; who needs an extra burden or responsibility? Why not accept the liturgical status quo, so easy, so pleasant, so flexible?

Despite an intellectual awareness that women have a different and objectively second-class status in the Orthodox synagogue, I still feel rather comfortable in that particular setting. Sometimes I prefer just to sit in the last row of the back section on my side of the *mehitzah*, the section with the latecomers, the young mothers with infants, the little children, and simply bask in the vitality and vibrancy of the place, an atmosphere so rich and thick with life and community that you almost can rub it between your fingers. There have been occasions, of course, when I've felt restless or remote, but these have been few and far between. More often than not, I am swept up into the vortex of this special community. Somehow, praying in an Orthodox synagogue is a refreshing experience each time.

And the *mehitzah!* Perhaps, because I am so used to it, this separation doesn't trigger resentment, as outsiders expect it would. Its ideal function is said to generate an aura of aloneness with God, the individual apart from family. In practice, the *mehitzah* also serves a social function; it contributes to community cohesiveness through the process of male and female bondings. I know most Orthodox women and men share these feelings, for hardly no one in the community is clamoring for change.

Finally, there is the dilemma that cannot be overlooked. Of the groups that have mandated equality of women in liturgy in modern times—Reform, Reconstructionist, Conservative—the fact is that neither men nor women pray with any sort of regularity. No, it's certainly not bad in the traditional community, the way things are. Still, I am driven to ask other questions, questions that lie at the rim of my contentment, that puncture the perimeter of my complacency. Do I really believe that women's communion is different in God's eyes and that He wants it any less? Are men truly more suited to a rigorous discipline of prayer, or is it simply that women have been given or have taken the easy way out?

And what about the spiral effect of release? Without actually assuming full and equal responsibility, will it ever be possible to have full and equal access—especially in a system that defines access in terms of responsibility? Can a woman ever hope to qualify for religious leadership if she has not met equal tests as a layperson? Indeed, is there not an inseverable link between release and restraint, between unaccountability and public invisibility, between ascribed junior status and reduced self-esteem? If we have learned anything at all from feminism, is it not that rights and responsibilities must come together?

What subtle side messages, I am forced to ask, have emerged all these centuries from women's partialness in liturgy? Second sex? Not full members of the community? Incapable of fixed responsibility? Not in control of time and destiny? Even if we were to say this was not the intent of the rabbis in interpreting women out of mainstream Jewish liturgical activities, we still would have to acknowledge the negative value judgments this spawned, generation after generation.

Finally, what about young women now growing up in the community, women who have neither ambivalence nor complacency, women who no longer will be satisfied with prayer by proxy and spiritual community at arm's length? What about women who have no man through whom to experience rituals vicariously—single women, widows, divorcées? How will the community respond to women who want to be held accountable and who expect to be fully counted? Even if there were no such women, I must ask myself, do I want my daughters to be conditioned to the same level of expectation as I was?

So, despite my complacency, I must conclude that repair, and not repetition, is the more worthy alternative, uphill though the struggle will be. Given the new reality of women today, it seems that this is perhaps the right moment in history to chart a more demanding spiritual course, to retrieve the obligation from its limbo state, to restore women to the sound habits of liturgy, and to give women equal status and equal access that comes with obligation. I believe it can be done in halakhic ways that are continuous with tradition: by educating Jewish women to their responsibilities, by shrinking the period of exemption so that it becomes one of function and not of blanket gender, and by reinterpreting women's status in the spiritual community.

Educating Women to the Mitzvah That Does Exist

It goes without saying that education is very important. Those women who pray do so by and large because they have been taught that way. But education has its limits. The fact is, it has worked only for very small numbers of women in the Orthodox community, or it works until a certain age, and then whatever it was that was learned becomes unlearned. More than education is needed.

Above all else, the exemption of women has had a powerful ripple effect. Resonating in every area, affecting feminine spiritual and intellectual responses far beyond its immediate legal reach, the exemption has undermined the best intentions, the finest educational efforts. Hence, the need to attenuate its effects. I can conceive of a halakhic process that starts by shrinking the period of exemption. Women, in general, will be included in the obligation of time-bound mitzvot (as they are in many instances) yet will be allowed an exemption during child-raising years, when the immediate, open-ended claims of child upon parent cannot be put off. Perhaps the exemption can be operative until a youngest child reaches seven, or ten, or twelve or thirteen, the latter being the ages that in Jewish tradition are synonymous with self-responsibility of the young (twelve for females, thirteen for males).

Perhaps it is not as formidable a halakhic leap as it seems. The very language of the exemption states that women are *patur* (exempt, dismissed). This summons up a primal obligation of all Israel, with women subsequently exempt. Perhaps such a ruling is no more than separating the essence of the covenant—to love God and to serve Him—from the various forms it has taken throughout history.

Maintaining the exemption for mothers of young, then, will achieve several things: halakhically, it will be more continuous with the past, and it will allay oft-voiced fears that *tefilah* would interfere with family tasks. More important, it will turn the categorical gender exemption from something negative for women, as it is now, to something more positive. It will make a subtle yet powerful statement about the holiness of raising a family, which for a few crucial years can take precedence over the mitzvah of prayer. The halakhic model is *ha-osek ba-mitzvah patur min ha-mitzvah*—one who is busy doing one mitzvah is exempt from another (Sukkah 25a). Stated in this manner, it may help create an awareness of the religious significance of child-care tasks and thereby attenuate the negative value assigned these tasks in society today.

It may be that reformulating the exemption for women in terms of function rather than gender may turn out to be an intermediate step, with the final step being exemption by function for either sex. As society moves slowly but inexorably toward a more equal sharing of child-care and household tasks, we begin to observe all kinds of social supports for men as fathers that were unimaginable a mere generation ago—things like paternity leave, the abolition of late-night meetings, and so on. It is not inconceivable, therefore, as part of the organic growth of Halakhah, that the exemption will fall to the father in Jewish families when he is the primary nurturer of the young. This is a logical conclusion of exemption by function.

In the meantime, however, weight must be given to tradition and history. We need to be properly sensitive to halakhic tradition and its rhythm as it attempts to funnel greater access and responsibility to women. To do otherwise at this moment is to polarize and destroy without achieving any additional real gains. Moreover, weight must be given to social reality and biology. Most women, I believe, will continue to want the edge on nurturing the young.

The most obvious effect of the inclusion of women under the obligation will be to make *tefilah* an appropriate, ongoing expression of commitment for a woman during the larger portion of her life, the first twenty or thirty years before she has children and her last thirty or forty years after her children are able to function independently.

I suspect we also will observe the following pattern. Once conditioned to pray, women will continue, even during those periods when they are halakhically exempt. Somehow, despite the open-ended nature of child care, women increasingly have assumed multiple roles that take them outside the home. I know a few women who work, who have sizable families, who are active in the community, and who also have never missed a *Shmoneh Esreh* in their lives, even during pregnancy, childbirth, and care of infants. Women also can learn from men, who somehow manage to meet their prayer obligations even during periods of increased pressure and responsibility.

Redefining Women's Status in Communal Prayer

Halakhically, the obligation to pray is quite independent of the obligation to pray in a minyan. Although law manages to separate the two, the psyche cannot; at some deeper level, public and private modes are inextricably woven. That there is a symbiotic relationship between communal and private prayer was well understood by the rabbis, who taught that if a man cannot pray with a minyan, he should synchronize his prayer with the minyan prayer times (Berakhot 7b–8a). Therefore, as reinforcement to a pattern of steady prayer, as a natural extension of it, and as a symbol of making amends regarding the public dignity of Jewish women, the halakhic obligation of women in public prayer should be instated, or reinstated, as the historic case may be.[14]

A vital distinction must be made regarding the exact nature of the obligation. Prayer in a minyan is "urgently preferable"; it is not "mandatory."[15] "Urgently preferable" means that a woman who takes her prayer obligations seriously will not necessarily be forced out into the public sector to pray with a minyan, just as a man is not mandated to recite all of his prayers with a minyan. On the other hand, when a woman does come together with other Jews for prayer, she ought to be considered a member of equal standing in the prayer community.

I have used the term "dignity." It is not insult or abuse or personal offense I speak of; Orthodox women simply don't feel that way, despite the fact that outsiders think we should. When I speak of the public dignity of women, I have in mind what seems just and proper, theologically as well as otherwise. My belief in the perfect God does not allow me to believe that God favors one sex over the other in constituting a holy congregation.

The synagogue is not a place of prayer alone. It is no accident that of the three Hebrew terms used to refer to "synagogue" (*bet midrash*—house of study; *bet tefilah*—house of prayer; *bet knesset* —house of gathering) the one that connotes community—*bet knesset*—preempts the other two. In Orthodox Jewish life today, the community orients itself around the synagogue. Given the fact that women live longer and show an increasing ability to move flexibly between private and public roles, the synagogue ought to be looking for ways to lay claim to a woman's time, presence, and energies, not to read her out. The truth is that rabbis and lay leaders do encourage women to participate in synagogue-related activities. The discrepancy, then, between their public presence and their halakhic nonstatus becomes even more glaring. When in the eighteenth century the Vilna Gaon instructed his daughters to pray at home rather than enter a synagogue, he drew upon an entirely different cultural and social reality. As Jewish women assume many new roles and as they increasingly achieve equal status in the broader society, should they not be accorded the same dignity in their primary community?

I know it is not a simple or easy thing to ask that contemporary halakhists search for means to integrate women into the minyan. For one thing, the fact that Reform, Reconstructionist, and Conservative Judaism acted first makes it difficult for the Orthodox even to consider the issue independent of its political overtones. This is regrettable but true. It also is difficult simply because most women will find the interim stage awkward and uncomfortable as they move from low profile to high visibility.

These two issues will have to be resolved in process. As internal pressure arises, interdenominational politics will diminish in importance. This may be called a sliding scale of religious politics. Similarly, only as women begin to experience heightened involvement will it feel less alien to them.

Numerous other questions will be raised. For example: What about women who do not take seriously the obligation but want only the rights? This question has several other ramifications. Herewith, two: "Once women are counted in the minyan and get their right to be called to the Torah, they won't even bother to show up"; or, "If women fall under obligation and don't fulfill it, this simply will create more transgressions in the world." To which one must reply with a question: If the power of a *hiyyuv* (obligation) is to bind, is it not just as likely that under obligation women will increase their observance, not decrease it, and that with greater rights women will assume more responsibility, not less? At the very least, a woman should be accorded the same benefit of doubt given a man. No one checks a man's tzitzit—that is, whether or not he has assumed full obligation for the six hundred and thirteen commandments. Nor are we required to check. We all know of countless instances where a "male Jewish body" is drafted off the streets to serve as the tenth man for a minyan, often simply to stand there and say "Amen"; this to the credit of the rabbis, who understood the primacy of *klal Yisrael,* of not writing off even the least of our brethren. And a fortiori for the woman who comes voluntarily, out of her own commitment.

Will a mixed gender destroy the *mehitzah*? Perhaps a century is too soon to tell anything about causal relationships, but the fact is that mixed seating was practiced long before there was any talk of equal obligations. Mixed seating, in part, reflects the Americanization of the synagogue; the issue of equality in communal prayer derives from a fundamental theological issue. If the *mehitzah* serves to maintain second-class status for women, it will become increasingly vulnerable as traditional women become more conscious and less passive about sexual hierarchies. I have been in synagogues where women could not hear the services, where they had to look cross-eyed to see what was going on. I have been in other places where the *mehitzah* made an altogether different statement about women, where it was constructed so that women could not only see and hear equally well but where the absence of women would have diminished noticeably the community feeling of prayer. It seems therefore that the *mehitzah* does not inherently demean women, nor must it fall away as women assume new roles, nor is "separate" in every last instance synonymous with "unequal."[16]

The *mehitzah* serves more than the spiritual and social functions mentioned above—an intimate aloneness with God and male and female bondings. It also undeniably highlights sex differentiation, no small feat in a society that sometimes confuses equality with androgyny. The mystery of human sexuality is far more pervasive in the *mehitzah* framework than in a synagogue with mixed seating, where sexuality simply is taken for granted. In fact, as I look about me on Shabbat morning, I find it hard to relate the original rationale for separate seating—that the presence of women may lead to frivolity—to the current reality. It just doesn't seem to fit. To the bare eye there appears to be less decorum and more camaraderie in a synagogue with a *mehitzah* than without. I'm not so sure that the rabbis didn't understand that sex bonding and a sense of human sexuality are positive factors in building up the chosen community.

All of this is not to say that separate seating necessarily is the only way, or the most pleasant way, for a Jew to pray. Still, there are aspects of it that are quite defensible. Furthermore, the halakhic politics of the community makes it highly inexpedient to link *mehitzah* with the equality of liturgical obligations and rights. The *mehitzah* nevertheless also should serve to remind us to remain vigilant lest it be used, as it has in the past, to perpetuate the second-class status of women in communal prayer.

A word is in order here about women's minyanim as a solution to the problem of peripheral status. A women's minyan does have considerable value, for in it a woman can acquire skills she otherwise would have no opportunity to develop: leading prayer, reading the Torah, even acquiring a familiarity with the order of *tefilot* that men routinely develop. Individual communities ought to help women to form prayer groups. It isn't easy to organize one and it's even harder to keep it going. The Riverdale women's *tefilah* group, in my own community, which consists mostly of married women with children culled from the three local Orthodox shuls, meets once a month in one of the synagogues and has the full support of the host rabbi and his congregation. Still, it has taken great time and effort of a few dedicated women to see it through its third year. Even now, the monthly Shabbat date often is determined according to which of two Torah portions has the least number of verses.

A women's minyan is an interim solution at best. A totally separatist solution is not what the covenantal community is all about.

Moreover, a separate minyan will continue to be satisfying only for a small number of women. For the majority, full access will have to come within the range of a full community. A synagogue naturally is a place that strengthens family, not divides it.

What about kaddish? Counting women when they come is one thing, but under equal obligation, a female mourner will be required to pray with a minyan three times a day. Kaddish raises a host of issues—women's security, family responsibilities, and even questions of which member of the family takes precedence in communal prayer. The year my husband said kaddish for his father, of blessed memory, our whole lives had to be restructured—not only wake-up times but meal and sleep times, work hours, travel, guests, everything. Never to have missed a single kaddish for eleven solid months, on top of a very full schedule, took planning and stamina. It was also one of the most incredible experiences of healing grief through the ties of a gentle and supportive community.

Could a woman do it? I know one woman who did and another who could. Recently, at a Monday-morning bar mitzvah, I met an old friend, a rabbi of substantial reputation and following, a man unalterably opposed to any changes regarding women and Halakhah. Knowing that I was a long-time admirer of his wife, the mother of eleven children, he explained to me with pride why she wasn't there. She was currently a full-time nursing intern, the only grandmother in the rigorous program. In order to avoid hospital duty on Shabbat, she worked an 8:00 A.M. shift every morning. That meant she had to leave the house at 6:30 A.M. each day. "And guess who makes the *cholent* every Friday?" he said with a twinkle in his eye.

Now I know that one energetic grandmother does not answer the question. But she does point up the fact that traditional women, so strongly associated with home and family, are also capable of disciplined responses outside the home. I couldn't help wonder silently whether my friend had made any connection between the rigorous diurnal regimen of his wife and his own narrow stand on women and Jewish tradition.

It will take family and community supports to enable a woman to fulfill the mitzvah of kaddish. Women involved in the more immediate religious task of nurturing young life would, of necessity, be released from the responsibility of honoring the dead. But the benefits of routinely including women in communal mitzvot may far outweigh the difficulties. I compare the lives of Ruth and Dan, who lost their spouses a few years ago. Ruth and her husband Irwin were founders of the synagogue and were active members for twenty years. After Irwin died it was as if the synagogue had no place for Ruth. Lately I've noticed that she's stopped coming. Dan, on the other hand, established even stronger synagogue ties after his wife died; daily minyan, which he had not attended before her death, became an important anchor in his life. It was not just the prayer, it was the group, the organizing principle. It's three years now, and he still goes to daily minyan.

There are some Jewish men who say kaddish with a minyan every day, as the Halakhah requires, others who say it when they can, and others who engage a third party to say kaddish for a loved one. Women surely can distribute themselves along the same continuum. Those women who take on the discipline of daily kaddish in a time of trauma will reap the psychological, spiritual, and kinship rewards the rabbis of ancient times formulated so brilliantly.

The Binding Force of Halakhah

Some people say to all of this, "Let women pray; who's stopping them? Let them say kaddish. Let them form their own prayer groups. Let them organize women's hakafot." And so on. But facts fly in the face of such ideas. Most Jewish women do none of these things. Neither would men if they did not feel the full, binding force of the obligation upon them. In that simple fact lies the fundamental truth and strength of halakhic Judaism. Jewish law addresses not the extraordinary or the supermotivated. It speaks to the average person and raises him or her to a different level. Were I, as a woman, not commanded to observe Shabbat and kashrut, I would do everything in my power to enable the men in my life carefully to observe these mitzvot, but I probably would feel unrestrained to take advantage of Saturday sales or to eat lobster and shrimp. I am so commanded, however, so even the mere thought of doing otherwise holds a certain revulsion for me.

Not only do I observe Shabbat and kashrut, but I have come to love these mitzvot and appreciate the many ways they define me as a Jew.

Given their general fidelity to Halakhah, it seems that the Orthodox have the most to gain from integrating feminist values. Who can translate better into Jewish terms ideas such as the "equal ability of women to rise to new expectations" than the group that has performed consistently well in halakhic expectations? It is not enough to say that there is nothing evil about the status quo; given the unique levers the halakhic system offers, one ought to say, "How much better it would be if women were interpreted in."

In the area of women and liturgy, perhaps more than any other sphere of ritual, we see the tremendous diversity of interpretation, reversals of earlier opinions, social expediencies interfaced with Sinaitic tradition. Simply to trace historical patterns—erratic to say the least—is to come away with the feeling that there was some element of human variability in halakhic interpretation. What happened, for example, between the second century, when the Mishnah taught that women are exempt from reciting the *Shema*, and the seventeenth century, when the *Shulhan Arukh* added that women nevertheless should be taught to accept the yoke of the heavenly kingdom (reciting the daily *Shema*); between the seventeenth century and the twentieth century, when no self-respecting religious educational system would allow its daughters *not* to say the *Shema*? Who can explain the history of rabbinic release of women from the mitzvah of lulav, or for that matter the medieval and modern halakhic acceptance, if not insistence, that women bless the lulav?

What happened between the original rabbinic release of women from shofar and the almost universal halakhic inclusion of women today, including the practice of going to the house of a woman who is unable to come to synagogue, in order to discharge her in the mitzvah of hearing the shofar, as is done for a man similarly confined?[17] And is there not clearly a rabbinic arbitrariness in the case of the grace after meals? The Torah tells us, "and you shall eat, be satisfied, and bless God" (Deut. 8:10). It does not distinguish anywhere between male and female in that commandment. The rabbis, however, determined that the grace obligation for women is not a commandment from the Torah but rabbinic in origin (*Piskei Ha-Rosh*, Berakhot 7:4).[18] Since women have a lesser source of obligation when men and women share the same table, women may not constitute the *zimmun* (the quorum of three males that convenes the grace). The laws of *zimmun* provide rich insight on how the male ritual hierarchy perpetuated itself. There was no element of fixed time, no question of public or private presence, no issue of mixed company. The whole *zimmun* takes but one minute and is recited responsively before the grace. Women are required to answer to men's *zimmun* or constitute one themselves if there are three women but not three men present. How then can we understand the notion of not permitting women to constitute with men a *zimmun*? It reflects, I think, the rabbinic will to preserve "community" as male. It was not difficult to find a halakhic way.

In sum, women were included in certain liturgical obligations because they routinely accepted and fulfilled certain mitzvot; in others, they were educated to more responsibility; in still others, as in daily prayer, they simply slipped away almost unnoticed; and finally, in some instances they arbitrarily were interpreted out. Thus, those who say "no change for women in liturgy" are themselves writing new rules about women and Halakhah. The task of religious leaders today is to find ways to balance the new moral and ethical judgments regarding women with the ritual aspects of Halakhah. It is not automatically to foreclose every opportunity to raise women to new levels of liturgical and communal involvement.

Just as exemption and public invisibility in the past have had a negative domino effect, so will responsibilities and full rights for women now ripple in a positive manner. One such area will be in the celebration of life events that are singularly female.

One of the beauties of Judaism is that nothing is taken for granted. Every act, every event, every new stage, every rite of passage becomes a religious experience that somehow binds up the individual with God and community. But this has been more true for men than for women. In the past, the communal and religious celebration of the birth of a boy or his entry into puberty has had no equivalent expression for females in our vast tradition. Is it not cause for reflection that in a religion so sensitive, so complete, where there is a blessing for everything—for thunder and lightning, for travel, for eating, for elimination, for new fruits and new clothes—that tradition has not formulated not even a single blessing, much less a full-blown ritual, to mark what surely is a peak moment in a woman's life? Imagine what a religious celebration Judaism would have developed by now had it been men who experienced the miracle of birth all these generations!

As women are encouraged to take their own spiritual capacities more seriously, they will begin to develop religious forms that express the emotions they feel in their hearts, emotions that currently find no particularist Jewish expression. After the initial stage of innovation and experimentation is over, these religious forms will find their way into the mainstream of tradition to enrich future generations.

A second result of shared liturgical responsibilities will be the sharing of communal leadership roles. At face value, leadership and liturgy seem unconnected. Still, I believe that women's lack of status in community prayer both dampened their interest and constricted their opportunities for responsible leadership roles, lay and religious, across the board of a structured community. Although the process already has begun to reverse itself, it will move along that much faster with positive models from every sector.

Finally, and most important of all, full responsibility and rights will bring women more readily to daily prayer, a difficult thing to come by in a society that does not pray naturally. Daily prayer sometimes is uplifting, sometimes routine, but it always is reflective of a Jewish commitment. Formalized prayer is a way of bringing into one's own time and place the awareness of God's creation, the miracles of our having been saved, the blessings of life and love that we enjoy, the existential concerns that escape not a single one of us. Prayer also is a way of uniting oneself with the Jewish people. Less sublime, and perhaps more immediate, it is a way of marking one's time as a Jew, and even in that there is great value.

A few years ago, on a Sunday afternoon, I drove to the ice-skating rink to pick up two of my children. I arrived a half-hour before the session ended, curious to know whether all those skating lessons had paid off. Instead, I was to learn something else. As I stood behind the glass window, I marveled at my fourteen-year-old son whiz around the rink with grace and speed, his thirteen-year-old sister trailing a little slower. Suddenly I noticed David get off the ice and stand near the empty spectators' benches. Seconds later, Deborah skated up to the side of the rink, watched him for a long moment, and continued on skating. As I pondered David standing there in his skates, barely moving, I filled up with pride. A moment ago he had blended perfectly with all the colorful skaters on the ice. Now, for a few brief moments, before darkness set in, David found it somewhere within him to separate himself, to project himself briefly onto another plane, to make a statement about being a Jew. Even if his afternoon prayer was hurried, it nevertheless had all the earmarks of *kedushah*, of holiness—separation, delineation, definition, commitment. What a remarkable religion, I thought. What power it has to compel a fourteen-year-old boy to rise to the moment or simply to touch base. Would that this power extended to girls, to mature women.

All of this is not to say that everything in Judaism need be identical for male and female. Gender-specific tasks can be quite healthy and pleasing, for women are not identical to men, nor must they be bound by perfectly parallel mitzvot. Yet prayer, like study, is such a large and significant part of a traditional Jew's life that to foster a climate that inhibits the flowering of women's prayer and learning is to cut off the nurturing forces in the life of a Jew, to reduce one's wholeness as a Jew, to weaken the links to past and future.

Distinct liturgical tasks for men and women thus will have to be drawn more carefully but not the global ones that we inherited—prayer, study, community for men; husbands, children, households for women. Perhaps the male-female distinctiveness will manifest itself in such divisions as candlelighting by women and havdalah by men, as is now the case; or the Purim megillah read by women and the Hanukkah candles lit by men; or kiddush chanted by a man and the *motzi* by a woman—lines that begin to approach and symbolize equality.

Whichever way the lines are drawn, the losses and the gains must be weighed. I do not think tallit and tefillin are the be-all and end-all of daily prayer; I still tend to think of them as male garb. Yet it would seem to me that a man who begins life each morning with these words, "And I betroth you unto eternity; I betroth Myself to you in lovingkindness and in mercy, in righteousness and in justice," as he wraps the tefillin about his head and arm, has a qualitatively different start on the day, even if he concentrates on the meaning of the words only once or twice a year. We will have to discover equivalent forms. Until such time, perhaps women will have to latch onto some of those ready-made obligations and rights that have served Jews so well for centuries.

NOTES

1. The contrast between men and women is quite sharp even in the Hasidic community, where prayer is elevated above all other religious duties. "It follows from the imagery of the Shekinah as female and the worshiper as male that women are not normally within the full scope of the Hasidic doctrines on prayer" (Louis Jacobs, *Hasidic Prayer* [Philadelphia: The Jewish Publication Society of America, 1973], p. 61).

2. On this "switch" see Eliakim Ellinson, *The Woman and the Mitzvot* (Hebrew), rev. ed. (Jerusalem: The Jewish Agency/Alpha Press, 1979), pp. 98–100.

3. According to the Tosafot of Rabbi Judah he-Hasid, this was not merely an interpretation of Maimonides but rather the text of the talmudic manuscript he had before him. See Ellinson, *Woman and Mitzvot*, p. 101, n. 5.

4. Rabbi Abraham Avli Gombiner, *Magen Avraham* 106:4, on Orah Hayyim.

5. Rabbi Israel Meier Hakohen (Hofetz Hayyim), Mishnah Berurah 106:4, on Orah Hayyim. Note also his inclusion of the *Shema*, another example of the flux on each issue; women technically were exempt from reciting the *Shema*.

6. *Arukh Hashulhan*, Orah Hayyim 106:7. Note here the slight variation: "three daily *tefilot*." Until now, all of the halakhists referred to women's obligation for only two daily prayers (morning and afternoon) and not for *maariv* (evening prayer). According to all views, *maariv* is voluntary and became obligatory upon men only because they accepted it as such. Since women never took it upon themselves, it never became obligatory.

7. See Ellinson, *Woman and Mitzvot*, chs. 3–5, for a fuller discussion of women performing mitzvot from which they originally were exempt.

8. *Sefer Abudraham*, The Third Gate, Blessings over the Commandments. There are several variations on this theme: "A woman was created to serve as helpmeet to her husband. . . . Man is to rule over woman . . . to teach her to follow his instructions" (Rabbi Jacob Anatoli, *Melamed ha-talmidim*, Parashat Lekh Lekha, cited in Ellinson, *Woman and Mitzvot*, p. 31).

9. Samson Raphael Hirsch, *Commentary on the Torah* (London: I. Levy, 1962), Lev. 23:43. Rabbi Aaron Soloveitchik also expressed this view in "The Jewish View of the Higher Nature of Women: And Thou Excellest Them All," *The Jewish Horizon* (November 1969). Hirsch in general had a most favorable attitude toward women and was one of the pioneers in education for women.

10. On this midrash see M. Meiselman, *Jewish Women in Jewish Law* (New York: Ktav, 1978), p. 45. Compare Ellinson, who uses the phrase "one heart" (single-mindedness) positively (i.e., to God's will). Ellinson also brings a commentary on the Yalkut Shimoni, which says the opposite—that women have one heart, the evil inclination that supersedes the good (*Woman and Mitzvot*, p. 32, n. 17). Rabbi Joseph Dov Soloveitchik once explained why slaves and minors are exempt from time-bound commandments: because they have no control over their own time and, therefore, over their own destinies; he did not explain why women also are included in that category (Yahrzeit Shiur, Spring 1977).

11. Saul Berman, "The Status of Women in Halakhic Judaism," *Tradition* 14 (Winter 1973): 5–28.

12. These consist of the *borkhu*, the *kaddish*, and the repetition of the *amidah* (the silent devotion) with the *kedushah*. In geonic times (ca. tenth century), the mourner's kaddish was added formally as a holiness passage that could be recited only in a quorum. The Torah and haftarah readings with accompanying blessings also are read only in the communal service. The laws of women and aliyot, however, are derived from another source, although the net effect is the same. See Abraham Milgram, *Jewish Worship* (Philadelphia: The Jewish Publication Society of America, 1971). On aliyot, see David Feldman, "Women's Role and Jewish Law," *Conservative Judaism* 26 (Summer 1972): 29–39.

13. There is no mention of gender in this talmudic description of a quorum; it simply states the number ten. The *Shulhan Arukh* is the first to mention ten men. On this and the "somewhat less than adequate" application of the *gezerah shavah* (the talmudic principle of like parts), see Phillip Sigal, "Women in a Prayer Quorum," *Judaism* 23 (Spring 1974): 177, n. 10.

14. Reform and Reconstructionist Judaism have mandated equal status for women in public prayer. The decision of the Rabbinical Assembly of Conservative Judaism in 1973 allowed for inclusion of women in a minyan. Local synagogue practice varies according to the decision of the local rabbi. The decision of the Conservative Law Committee was based on the halakhah that the primary obligation for prayer is public prayer. Since women were not excluded explicitly, rabbinically they must be considered included in the public worship obligation. See especially Sigal, "Women in a Prayer Quorum," pp. 174–82.

15. Meiselman, *Jewish Women*, uses the term "urgently preferable" (p. 134); Sigal, "Women in a Prayer Quorum," calls it a "mandatory mitzvah of high priority." Meiselman's term is a more solid base upon which to bridge the gap between taking account of women in public prayer and not obligating them to be there when other factors do not warrant it.

16. Two New York synagogues whose construction reflects the new view of women and community are The Hebrew Institute of Riverdale and Lincoln

Square Synagogue. In an eloquent defense of the opposite view (that, ipso facto, separate is unequal), see Cynthia Ozick, "Notes toward Finding the Right Question," *Lilith* (Fall 1979).

17. See also Arlene Pianko, "Women and Shofar," *Tradition* 17 (Fall 1974): 54–67.

18. See Berakhot 20b, 45b; Arakhin 3a. Tosafot, on Berakhot 20b, offers this basis of interpretation: One verse in the grace refers to "the covenant which Thou hast signed in our flesh (circumcision), the Torah which Thou hast taught us." Since neither of these apply to women, women cannot enable one to whom circumcision and Torah do apply to fulfill his obligation. By arbitrariness, I mean that the rabbis might have ruled just as easily that since women also eat and are sated and bless God, they are obligated equally, even though one verse of the grace does not apply to them. After all, grace is a positive commandment that is not time-bound.

In Defense of the "Daughters of Israel": Observations on Niddah and Mikveh

A Very Private Affair

SEVERAL years ago, on a June evening, my husband and I left our children in the care of a baby-sitter and went out for two hours. I had told the baby-sitter and Moshe, the only child still awake at that hour, that we were going shopping. I knew that Moshe would be asleep by the time we returned, so there was no question of having to deal with the natural inquisitiveness of a six year old. I also knew that Patti, our baby-sitter, the teenage daughter of our Irish Catholic neighbors, was too well bred to inquire why I had come back from shopping with no packages but with a headful of long, wet hair.

It was not that I was ashamed to talk about mikveh, the ritual bath. But because the subject is so fraught with modesty and taboo, I would have preferred to avoid it. What I didn't anticipate upon our return was to find an old friend who had stopped by the house. Carol and I had been in graduate school together for four years. She knew a little about Jewish life; her grandparents had been Orthodox. Unlike some people of their liberal, intellectual background, Carol and her husband were not antagonistic toward Judaism. On the contrary, while they would have none of Shabbat, kashrut, synagogue life, or day-school education for themselves or their son, they were nevertheless quite respectful of our way of life.

Carol has an incredible mind. Anything she had ever read or heard was tucked away in some crevice of memory, to be recalled instantly at the proper moment. Somewhere in the past, maybe in her brief bout with Hebrew school fifteen years earlier, she had heard about mikveh. Thus, she was able to put it all together immediately—wet hair, street clothes, no packages—and come up with an answer. The moment the baby-sitter closed the door behind her, Carol blurted out, "Do you really practice *that?* Do you actually go to the . . . the mikveh?"

For the first time in my life I had the feeling that someone was seeing me as some kind of aborigine disguised in twentieth-century garb. I found myself at a loss for words. It was a subject that lay very quiet and deep inside of me. I then had been married for ten years. No one had ever asked me why I observed the laws of niddah. (Niddah, it should be noted, has several meanings, depending on the context: the laws pertaining to niddah; the state of being sexually unavailable; that time of month that includes menstrual flow and after-period; a woman in a state of niddah.) I had never even asked myself the question or discussed it with my parents, sisters, or friends, not even with my husband, who observed the practice with me. In fact, the closest I had come to a discussion of the matter was when a high-school friend confided that her mother said she felt like a bride each month after going to the mikveh. It embarrassed me that a mother could make so suggestive and revealing a disclosure to a daughter, and for the rest of my impressionable teen years I could not look at that pious woman without a headful of immodest imaginings.

It wasn't that I didn't know the laws or the ancient and contemporary meanings attached to them. I had read many of the "little books" on the subject; they succeeded in neither frightening me nor inspiring me. Being a good "daughter of Israel"—the phrase is a euphemism for one who observes the laws of niddah and mikveh—it never occurred to me that I would do anything other than keep the particular practice. Just as my mother and mother-in-law went to some vague "meeting" once a month, there was no doubt that I too would carry on the chain of tradition. But like many such things, I took the whole matter of mikveh for granted. I had managed to appropriate intact its grand claims, but I had no sense of what positive meaning it had for me. Nor could I articulate what I was doing or thinking during those occasional times— and there were such—when it was a hardship or a nuisance for me to observe this mitzvah.

I think I mouthed some clichés to Carol and then quickly changed the subject. In time, Carol went on to become a well-known psychoanalyst, was divorced, remarried, and divorced again. The last I heard, she was making a fortune in private practice in Los Angeles and writing a book. I haven't seen her for fifteen years, but once a month, as I comb out my wet hair in the mikveh, I chuckle inwardly as her astounded expression passes before my eyes. Over the years, I have begun to sort out some of my feelings about this mitzvah, so powerful that it manages to control and make a statement about a human drive that everywhere else no longer seems to be subject to boundaries established by law, culture, or even family values.

The mikveh, as we all know, has come under attack by Jewish feminists, not-so-Jewish feminists, and not-so-feminist Jews. Carol didn't say so, but she probably thought to herself, "Mikveh. Ahah! 'Primitive blood taboo.' Outmoded and demeaning notions of 'unclean and impure'!" Perhaps some of these elements at one time or another were associated with the concept of niddah. Today they hold no weight, however, at least not for me nor, I believe, for most of the women who lovingly or reflexively take upon themselves the obligation. Besides, one just as easily could defend niddah in terms of its function in a prefeminist society. For example, niddah was intended to protect women's selves and sexuality; not bad, considering that society was oriented to the female serving the male, sexually and otherwise. Niddah also provided safeguards against women becoming mere sex objects; even when the law could not change social perceptions, at least it minimized those times when this attitude could be acted upon. Finally, the Talmud gives the most functional view of all, sexist though the language may seem today: "Because a man may become overly familiar with his wife, and thus repelled by her, the Torah said that she should be a niddah for seven clean days [following menses] so that she will be as beloved [to him after niddah] as on the day of her marriage" (Niddah 31b).

The Law and Its Practice

The Bible lays down the initial principles of physical separation during menses:

> When a woman has a discharge, her discharge being blood from her body, she shall remain in her impurity seven days; whoever touches her shall be unclean until evening. (Lev. 15:19)[1]

> Do not come near a woman during her period of uncleanness to uncover her nakedness. (Lev. 18:19)[2]

> If a man lies with a woman in her infirmity and uncovers her nakedness, he has laid bare her flow and she has exposed her blood flow; both of them shall be cut off from all the people. (Lev. 20:18)

In the rabbinic explication of biblical tradition, we find that the minimum niddah period increases from seven to twelve days[3]— that is, a five-day minimum allotted for the flow and seven days for the "whites," the additional days of separation.[4] (A word about the use of the term "whites": I do not like the term seven "clean" days, which all of the English sources employ, for it evokes its counterpart, "unclean." I therefore prefer "whites," which is the literal translation of the talmudic *levanim*, the white garments that women were required to wear during those seven days in order to facilitate the search for stains.) If the flow or the staining lasts longer than five days,[5] the seven-day "white" count begins after the last day of flow.[6] The whole cycle is completed with immersion.[7] This is known as *tevilah*. Afterward, a woman can resume sex until the next menstruation, some two and a half weeks later. The *tevilah* is also attended by numerous details. Unless there are extenuating circumstances, the immersion takes place in the evening, after dark, at the completion of the twelfth day.

As for the mikveh itself, there are numerous laws concerning the mikveh and its construction. In fact, a whole tractate of the

Mishnah (Mikvaot) is devoted to the subject. Briefly, the mikveh must be nonporous, so that it has no object than can absorb *tum'ah* (impurities). It is to be constructed of two compartments: *bor ha-otzar* (the storage compartment) and *bor ha-tevilah* (the immersion basin that is drained each day). The word *mikveh* simply means a collection (of water). This must be stationary water, not flowing, as from a tap, and its sources must be natural—rain water, wells, natural ice, or ocean or lake water. As the ancient rabbis were of a practical nature, however, and since it would be difficult to collect all that water naturally, they legislated that only a certain percentage of these natural waters is required to constitute a kosher mikveh; the rest may be made up from regular tap or drawn water. A lake or ocean may be used for the purpose, although there is halakhic concern that out of fear of such waters the immersion will not be performed properly.

Since the destruction of the Second Temple, the mikveh has been used primarily for women, but there are other uses for it as well. Some men go to the mikveh to purify themselves before certain holidays, particularly Yom Kippur. Mikveh is also the final step in conversion to Judaism. Many traditional Jews also immerse their new utensils in the mikveh before using them. For these other purposes, the mikveh is used only during the day. You will never see a man about the mikveh at night. The men who accompany their wives to the mikveh—and this is often the case—sit in their cars parked down the street aways.

In the Mikveh

If you have never been to a mikveh, this is what to expect. First you are asked whether you want a "private" or a "semiprivate." Private means that the mikveh basin (a small, deep pool) is in the same room where you bathe in a regular tub to prepare for the immersion; semiprivate and shower mean that you bathe or shower in your room but must go into an adjacent room to use the mikveh basin. Depending on the construction of the semiprivate, it can be like playing musical doors—all doors that lead to the mikveh basin are closed before your door is opened—so that you will have complete privacy while immersing. Before the bath, you brush your teeth, rinse your mouth, trim your nails, and remove all makeup, dentures, rings—anything that is not part of the body. After the bath, you rinse off in the shower, or just the latter if you have already bathed at home that evening. (This elaborate ritual of cleansing, incidentally, is further proof that the mikveh has nothing to do with personal hygiene or cleanliness.) You comb out your hair, which you have just shampooed, and wrap yourself in a white sheet or towel. Then you press the buzzer, which summons the "mikveh lady."

Mikveh ladies come in several varieties. I have been to a dozen different mikvehs over the last twenty years, and each mikveh lady has her own style. They are generally sensitive, devout women who are kind but not prying. They have a rather pleasant, quiet, businesslike manner that is exactly called for in so personal a situation. Occasionally, you will run across a mikveh lady who has some idiosyncracies, such as entering your room without knocking to see if you are ready, or one who will fight you over another sixteenth of an inch of your carefully trimmed fingernails, or even one who, without any warning whatsoever, will run a comb through your pubic hair while you stand there in total shock. In all fairness, however, these are the sum total of grievances I've heard concerning mikveh ladies over the years.

The mikveh lady checks to see if you have prepared yourself properly (trimmed nails, etc.). She looks you over to see if there are any loose hairs on your body, which she gently removes. Holding on to the side of the rail, you walk down a few steps to the bottom of the mikveh—the water is about shoulder height. With legs slightly part, lips and eyes closed but not clenched tightly, arms spread a bit at your sides but not touching the side walls, you bend your knees in a crouching position and go completely under. If you have long hair you have to go a little deeper, so that every strand of hair will be under water. You don't have to stay under the water for even an extra second. All you have to do is immerse yourself completely and then come right up. If you've done it right (every bit of you below the water line) your mikveh lady will pronounce it "kosher."

Then, standing there in the water, you recite the blessing:

Barukh ata adonai eloheinu melekh ha-olam asher kideshanu be-mitzvotav ve-tzivanu al ha-tevilah (Blessed are You O Lord, our God, King of the Universe, who has sanctified us by His commandments and commanded us concerning immersion). Other blessings are often added, the most common one being the *yehi ratzon*: "May it be Your will O Lord, our God and God of our fathers, that the Temple be speedily rebuilt in our time; give us our portion in Your Torah, so that we may serve You with awe as we did in days of old. And we shall offer to You the thanks offering of Judea and Jerusalem as was done in years gone by."[8] Many women cover their heads with a terry cloth, which the mikveh lady hands them, before saying the blessing. (It does seem rather incongruous, covering one's head in modesty and respect when all the rest of you is standing there stark naked. But that's how it is often done.)

After the blessings, you dip under two more times; each time, the mikveh lady pronounces it "kosher." Then you come up the steps, and she wraps a white sheet around you and leaves the room for you to dress. Before you leave, you pay a mikveh fee that ranges from three to ten dollars. (In no way does the fee cover the cost of running the mikveh, which is heavily subsidized by the community.)

A bride is brought to the mikveh a day or two before her wedding. There are some slight variations in custom, but the basic procedures are the same. Sephardim make a real celebration of the event, their equivalent to the bride's shower. Among Ashkenazim, it's pretty quiet, strictly a mother-daughter affair.

Most of the mikvehs today are quite pleasant places, especially the newer ones, built with the modern woman's tastes in mind. All mikvehs have hair dryers. Some even have beauticians and cosmeticians in attendance several evenings a week. The next stage will probably be whirlpools, saunas, and exercycles. And why not? It loosely fits the concept of *hiddur mitzvah*, the beautification of a mitzvah. No more the image of the mikveh for middle-aged rebbetzins only. I have seen women leaving the mikveh looking as if they had just stepped out of the pages of *Vogue*. Rabbi Akiba— who believed that women should use cosmetics and make themselves attractive (even during their menstrual period), so that they not become repulsive to their husbands—would have been proud!

The Historical Development of the Laws of Niddah

The laws of niddah provide us not only with an elaborate "how-to" but also with a fascinating lesson of the way in which Halakhah develops, for the precepts can be traced from the Bible, through the Mishnah, the Tosephta, the two Talmuds, and medieval and modern rabbinic literature.

The biblical commandment of separation during menses occurs in two different contexts: laws dealing with other forms of defilement, impurity, and death; and laws regulating forbidden sexual relations. Thus, at the outset, we encounter the two themes that are associated with niddah—themes that are reflected in Halakhah throughout history—sometimes intertwined, sometimes overshadowed, sometimes parallel.

As for the defilements and impurities mentioned in the Bible, these generally are related to death: contact with a dead body, loss of menstrual blood, loss of semen through nocturnal emission, or leprosy (all symbolic of the rampant forces of death taking over as the life-giving juices that nurture body tissue mysteriously cease). Purification through the living waters, then, symbolizes a renewal, a re-creation, a regeneration of the life forces.[9] As such, purification was considered a privilege, not a burden. To concretize this, there was a tangible communal reward: access to the sanctuary (and, later, the Temple), where one could bring a sacrifice and find oneself in the presence of God, who gives life. One who did not undergo a purification rite could not reenter the sanctuary.

The second association is that of family purity. (In fact, the laws of niddah are known as *taharat ha-mishpahah,* the laws of family purity.) The ancient, eternal truth is that society will destroy itself if it lacks ethical sexual relationships. Although no explicit reason is given for forbidding relations during menses, clearly this falls into the category of curbing liaisons that are most open to exploitation or that are most typical of animal rather than human behavior: incest, sex with individuals who live under the same roof but who are not each other's partners, sex with animals. For these forbidden liaisons, a punishment of *karet* was meted—a cutting off of the soul of the transgressor from the community.

After the destruction of the Second Temple, the categories of *taharah* and *tum'ah* (pure and impure) become almost irrelevant to daily life. In Eretz Israel, certain practices were to be maintained because of the holiness of the land, but gradually even these died out. This does not mean that the rabbis of the Talmud ceased discussing these concepts and their practical implications; it does signify, however, that all other forms of *taharah* and *tum'ah* were essentially inoperative: vessels, tents, hands, liquids, etc. Thus, because there was no longer a Temple where purity had to be preserved, a person who came into contact with a dead body no longer had to undergo ritual immersion. The only vestige of this practice remaining today is the washing of hands after leaving a funeral parlor or cemetery. More germane to our concern, a man who had a bodily discharge no longer had to abstain from sex until he underwent purification. The only person still subject to purification rites is the menstruous woman.

Following the destruction of the Temple, the emphasis shifted from *tum'at niddah* (separation for reasons of defilement, impurity, pollution, and taboo) to *issur niddah* (proscription of a sexual relationship because it is forbidden by Jewish law). Still, the whole area of niddah never completely lost its association with impurity and defilement.[10] Indeed, the rabbis strengthened the "fence" around the original prohibition. Sometimes they built on one base, sometimes on the other, often connecting the two.

The talmudic discussion in Shabbat 13a is a perfect example. The pericope opens with an invitation to "come and see how purity has increased in Israel" (in rabbinic times). The scholars ask: may a niddah sleep in bed with her husband, each fully clothed, thus avoiding bodily contact? Shammai answers in the affirmative—they may sleep together fully clothed, for sleeping together (during the "white" days) is not prohibited, only intercourse. Hillel disagrees —and the law is according to Hillel.

In this discussion, several analogies are drawn as proofs: some evoke defilement, others the restrictions on proper sex relations. One is treated in this passage to a taste of Halakhah in process. The discussion takes place after the minimum day count was increased from seven days (biblical) to twelve (five menses plus seven "whites"); initially, only intercourse was forbidden during the seven "whites," but at some point in the rabbinic period, probably around the time of Hillel and Shammai (first century B.C.E.), the biblical taboo against any and all forms of bodily contact during menses was carried over to the seven "whites" as well. The elusive biblical concept, that impurity could be transmitted by contact by touching, was dropped from every other category, yet increased in the case of niddah.

Similarly, the biblical punishment for infraction of niddah was intensified, and *karet* was extended to include the seven "whites." As we read in Shabbat 13a-b:

> [It is taught in the] Tanna de-be Eliyahu: It once happened that a certain scholar who had studied Bible and Mishnah and had unstintingly served scholars, died at middle age. His wife took his tefillin and carried them about in the synagogue and school houses and complained to them [the scholars]: "It is written in the Torah, 'For that is thy life and the length of thy days' (Deut. 30:20). My husband, who read much Bible and studied much Mishnah and served scholars a great deal, why did he die at middle age?" No man could answer. On one occasion I [Eliyahu, the supposed author of the Tanna] was a guest at her house, and she related the whole story to me. I said to her: "My daughter, how was he to you in the days of your menstruation?" "God forbid," she replied, "he did not even touch me with his little finger." "And how was he in the days of your 'whites'?" "He ate with me, drank with me, and slept with me in bodily contact, and it did not occur to him to do otherwise." I said to her: "Blessed be the Omnipresent for slaying him, for He did not condone this behavior. Therefore, even though the man had much merit on account of his love for the Torah, God punished him, for lo, the Torah has said, 'And you shall not approach a woman as long as she is impure by her menses' (Lev. 18:19)."

The Mishnah refers to an institution that undoubtedly grew out of the defilement concept. *Bet ha-tum'ot* (special houses of uncleanness) were set aside so that women could be segregated during menses.[11] This isolation was not practiced in Babylonia during the mishnaic period, however.[12] As is written in Ketubbot 61a:

> Rabbi Isaac ben Hanania further stated in the name of Rav Huna: All kinds of work which a wife may perform for her husband, a menstruous woman may also perform, except for filling his cup, preparing his bed, washing his face, hands, and feet. Said Rabba: The prohibition for preparing his bed applied only in his presence. If done

in his absence, it doesn't matter. With regard to filling his cup, Samuel's wife made a change [during her "whites"]; she served him with her left hand.

In other words, actions that were circumscribed biblically for reasons of defilement, such as touching the husband's bed, were now, in third-century Babylon, circumscribed for reasons of sexual arousal.

Variations showed up in attitudes as well as practice. The author of the following talmudic statement sounds a negative note: "If a menstruous woman passes between two [men] during the beginning of her menses, she will slay one of them; and if she is at the end of her menses, she will cause strife between them" (Pesahim 111a). Another talmudic passage (Niddah 31b) stresses the romantic element: a niddah is off limits so that she will be more desirable afterward.

And so it goes. The medieval literature largely emphasizes the pollution theme. The Zohar, with its almost palpable sense of purity and impurity in the world, is most explicit:

One who cohabits with a niddah drives the divine presence from the world. There is no stronger impurity in the world than that of niddah. Wherever they go, the divine presence is driven from before them. Furthermore, such a person brings evil sickness upon himself and upon the child born [from such a union]. . . . When a person draws near to a niddah, her impurity passes to him and resides in all of his limbs . . . for it is written: "and her impurity will be upon him" (Lev. 15:24). The seed which he brings forth at that time is imbued with the spirit of impurity and remains in a state of impurity throughout its existence, for its very creation and foundation stem from profound impurity, which is the strongest of all impurities. (Parshat Shmot)

We find a similar view in Nahmanides:

The glance of a menstruous woman poisons the air. . . . She is like a viper who kills with her glance. How much more harm will she bring to a man who sleeps with her? She is a pariah; men and women will distance themselves from her and she will sit alone and speak to no one. . . . The dust on which she walks is impure like the dust defiled by the bones of the dead. And the rabbis said: "Even her glance brings harm." (*Commentary on the Torah*, Lev. 12:14)

Maimonides, however, for all that he believed that women be kept under wraps, was of a different mind regarding isolation. The Babylonian tradition of setting women aside to prevent them from their normal household duties, was, in his eyes, inauthentic to rabbinic tradition; it smacked of sectarian extremism, perhaps even the most dreaded sectarianism of all, Karaism. Thus Maimonides permitted women to touch a garment, cook foods, and generally serve their husbands at all times (*Mishneh Torah*, Hilkhot Issurei Biah 11:6, 7, 15).

In medieval Spain, where Christianity stressed the sinfulness of sex and Islam played up the taboo, there arose some additional prohibitions in Jewish law. One in particular, the interdiction against a niddah entering a synagogue, was widely observed.

With the beginning of the modern period comes a new phenomenon, an attempt to provide a rationale for niddah in terms that would be more appealing to the enlightened mind. Thus, as Samson Raphael Hirsch writes, "in the proper marital relationship, husband and wife must live periodically as sister and brother. This tends to establish rather than curtail intimate family relationships, both morally and spiritually. And just as one gains entry to the holy sanctuary after purification, so one is able to resume sexual relations, which are also of a consecrated nature."[13]

In the contemporary literature on niddah, we see the dual influence. Some authorities stress impurity, defilement, punishment, danger, and various minute details, the neglect of which entails absolute infraction of the law; others emphasize married love, mutual respect, the holiness of sex, and the temptations that are involved when two people live in such close proximity.[14]

Often in contemporary literature these themes are meshed. Thus today, for example, strict observance of niddah means that there be absolutely no physical contact between husband and wife, that their beds be separated, that they do not hand any object to each other directly. One prominent halakhic authority states that even a baby is not to be handed directly (from husband to wife) during niddah, unless there is no other way. While it is possible to explain laws of this sort as safeguards against sexual arousal, they seem to be more evocative of biblical concepts of impurity, where, for example, a man who touches the chair or bed or clothing of one who is *tamei* (unclean) becomes unclean himself. Yet, there is also the other genre of prohibitions: a man should not gaze excessively upon his wife; a woman should not sing in the presence of her husband. In other words, everything must be done to bank all the potential fires of passion.

One Woman's Contemporary View

Relatively few Jews observe the laws of niddah today, not the great mass of assimilated Jews who ignore mitzvot in general, nor Reform Jews who view niddah as a relic of rabbinic Judaism, nor Conservative Jews who default by silence, nor, for that matter, many Jews who consider themselves Orthodox. And yet, the laws of niddah and mikveh are considered *gufei ha-torah*, the essential laws of the Torah. Mikveh, for instance, takes precedence in communal efforts over building a synagogue or buying a Torah scroll. Moreover, observance of niddah is one of the three primary mitzvot of women, the other two being *nerot* (the kindling of candles) and *hallah* (taking off a portion of the bread dough and consecrating it) (Berakhot 20b). Why then has niddah fallen by and large into desuetude?

One explanation is that niddah is simply very difficult to keep. Of all the core mitzvot, it certainly makes the most rigorous demands. Sex is as powerful a drive as hunger, yet we have only five fast days a year compared with approximately one hundred fifty days of niddah. One not trained to observe the law would hardly consider it.

Some would say that niddah and mikveh have fallen afoul of brass plumbing, the arch symbol of modern civilization. Too many people confuse the laws of niddah with hygiene. Indeed, how often have I heard people say, "I can just as easily stay home and take a bath." This kind of thinking is due in part to an inadequate education on the subject, including the simple fact that one is required to take a bath *before* going to the mikveh. It is also probably due to the use of words like "clean" and "unclean," which might not have crept into Jewish tradition had women been part of the process of the rabbinic unfolding of the law during the last

ON WOMEN AND JUDAISM | 118

two thousand years. The Torah deals with concepts of spiritual purity and impurity that were amorphous and perhaps logically incomprehensible, even in Temple times. But once the Temple was destroyed and there was no longer a single physical locus of ultimate purity, the human mind transmuted these concepts into terms with which it could deal. Somehow, relative cleanliness became the code association.

A further fact that contributed to the growing disregard of niddah is that all throughout the medieval period the notion of taboo overpowered the element of *kedushah*, the holiness of the physical relationship. Of course, taboo and holiness are tied together intimately—that is, the setting up of limits so that what happens within them becomes very special. The preponderant focus, however, on what not to do during the niddah period— combined with little discussion or appreciation of what takes place during the time when sex is permissible—left the whole area quite vulnerable. Instead of giving post-niddah sex the green light, in the form of positive articulation, the laws, as they developed, continued to give sex the red light. This is seen most clearly in the *Shulhan Arukh*, which prescribes sex to be kept at a minimum. A certain prudishness was generated here, not to be confused with modesty. It is interesting to note that *onah* (the obligation of a husband to satisfy his wife sexually), an equally important concept in the Torah, has found little stress in Jewish tradition. Thus, as modern men and women became increasingly disenchanted with taboos, niddah suffered accordingly. This falloff is unfortunate, for niddah and mikveh have great meaning today, in a woman's life and in the shared life of a man and woman who love each other.

Why do I observe niddah and mikveh? Because I am so commanded, because it is a mitzvah ordained by the Torah. Were I not so commanded by Jewish law, I surely would not have invented such a rigorous routine. The flesh is weak and no lofty scheme imaginable could have made me tough enough to observe niddah. All of this is true for my husband as well, for neither of us could adhere to the practice unilaterally. Without a mutual understanding and acceptance of Halakhah, observance of niddah in marriage would be reduced to a test of wills each month.

Precisely because it is a mitzvah, it holds a certain sense of sweetness for me. As I go about my business at the mikveh, I often savor the knowledge that I am doing exactly as Jewish women have done for twenty or thirty centuries. It is a matter not only of keeping the chain going, but also one of self-definition: this is how my forebears defined themselves as Jewish women and as part of the community and this is how I define myself. It is the sense of community with them that pleases me. There is yet another aspect to observing a mitzvah for its own sake. The laws of niddah continually remind me that I am a Jew and niddah reinforces that deep inner contentment with a Jewish way of life.

Acceptance of the mitzvah, then, is the base; attendant sensations of "community," "Jewish womanhood," and "chain of tradition" are the embellishments. There is more to it than that, however. Niddah serves a whole range of functions in an interpersonal relationship, appropriate to its ebb and flow and to its different stages of growth.

In the early married stage, when passion and romance dominate, niddah allows, nay encourages, a man and woman to develop other techniques of communication. In the second stage, that of young children, tired mothers, and hardworking fathers, niddah is an arbitrarily imposed refresher period. Inasmuch as it regulates the off times, it synchronizes the on times. No law can program desire, but there is probably a better chance of the meshing of expectations among couples who observe niddah. In the third stage, as a woman approaches menopause, niddah and mikveh bring her to a monthly appreciation of her continuing ability to be fertile. One may wonder whether a woman who has faithfully observed mikveh all her life feels a heightened sense of loss at menopause.

Finally, in all of these stages, niddah generates a different sense of self for a woman, a feeling of self-autonomy. Some women can generate these feelings out of their own ego strength; for those to whom it is not innate or instinctive, niddah is a catalyst to this consciousness.

Some feminists have challenged the very concept of mikveh. Yet mikveh well could be the prototype of a woman's mitzvah. It is unique to woman; it makes a statement about woman as Jew; it builds human character. Thus we need not rationalize what has been wrong with mikveh but rather affirm what has been right and

what is doable. Not everything concerning women that has withstood the test of time is good; not everything from biblical tradition
has withstood the test of time. But in the cosmic order of things,
mikveh seems to be an attempt to attach some measure of holiness
to a primal urge. As it was passed on through countless generations, mikveh could not help take on certain nuances, some of
them less honorable toward women. It falls to this generation of
women, Jewish women with a new sense of self, to restore that
element of holiness to our bodies, our selves.

Some Modest Proposals

There are several things regarding niddah and mikveh the community can do in the way of education and even refinement.

1. Niddah and mikveh should be reappropriated in the context of
a woman's mitzvah. Uniquely, it is a mitzvah in which women perform the act, with men serving as enablers. Now that women are
calling for greater inclusion in tradition, the first step should be to
reeducate the community on women's mitzvot that already exist.

2. There should be a clearing up of some of the negative language associated with niddah and mikveh—"unclean" for example
—and of some of the horrendous threats that have been bruited
about (children conceived during a niddah's intercourse will be
born blind, leprous, armless, etc.). That doesn't impress people
who prefer to take on new obligations out of love, not terror.
While much of the contemporary, English-language literature does
stress *kedushah*, the holiness of marriage and family purity, the
new literature should emphasize the holiness of sex itself. Indeed,
the parallel ought to be drawn: a man who goes to the mikveh
before Yom Kippur purifies himself not from a state of defilement
but rather in order to be more holy for what he does next (that is,
entering holy time). Similarly, menstrual blood is not defilement;
rather, after a period of separation a woman purifies herself to be
more holy for what follows, sexual relations.

3. Perhaps some of the women's contemporary needs can be
grafted onto niddah. For example, doctors advise women to check

their breasts every month for cancer, but most women neglect these self-examinations. If this were somehow tied halakhically to niddah, women would do so routinely. Similarly, an annual Pap smear or gynecological examination that would be tied ritually to, say, the first niddah cycle after Rosh Hashanah may add new meaning to the mitzvah; more than that, it may save thousands of women's lives each year.

4. At certain stages of life, and for certain people, abstention from sex for almost half a month is too difficult to sustain. Perhaps there ought to be a halakhic reconsideration of the biblical time span. At this time of return to ritual and tradition, many more Jewish couples seriously may consider the observance of niddah were it limited to the seven-day period prescribed by biblical law.

5. Particularly where brides are concerned, and on the assumption that we still place a value on virginity before marriage, the distinction between menstrual blood and blood of the hymen ought to be made. Starting off with eleven days of abstinence is a poor way to engender healthy attitudes about the joys of sex in marriage.

6. One of the interesting things that turned up in the course of my research on modern Orthodox women is the diversity in observance of the associated laws of *negi'ah*, the interdiction against all physical contact. Many couples seem to have drawn the line differently, and the range was enormous. As one who respects the mitzvah of niddah—but also as a student of history who understands that after the destruction of the Temple the emphasis quite naturally shifted from *tum'at niddah* (separation for reasons of ritual impurity) to *issur niddah* (proscription of sexual relations)—I find the emphasis on *negi'ah* excessive and onerous. Today we have somewhat healthier attitudes about physical affection. The Halakhah should reflect a confidence in its faithful. One who observes the mitzvah of niddah will not jump into bed the moment the flesh of a loved one is pressed.

Like many *hukkim* from the Torah (rituals and rules for which we are given no ethical or logical reason), niddah has come down to us through three thousand years of Jewish living. It has been tempered and shaped by successive generations, yet it remains relatively intact, faithful to its original, divine, biblical form. And although we cannot understand it by means of logic, it obviously serves a deep human need.

All things considered, the laws of niddah have added a dimension to our marriage, have made it richer, more special. Since it is these small margins that make the difference in life, I consider the effort worthwhile. All in all, I like being a proper "daughter of Israel."

NOTES

1. "Uncleanness" is a dreadful word, a poor translation and even poorer connotation of the Hebrew *tamei*. I could not find a single English Bible that used a different word, however. *Tamei* is more accurately understood as "impure"—the reverse condition of *tahor* ("pure"); both words take on an entirely different meaning when considered in light of Temple access or worship, to which they are related. Part of the problem in this pericope is that the word *niddatah* (her state of being niddah) is translated as "her impurity," so another word had to be used for *tum'ah*. More properly, *niddatah* should have been translated as "in the time of her flow (menses)" or "in the time of her separation (distancing)." Even where the concept of separation is used, some translators use the word "banishment," based on Rashi's commentary of Lev. 15:19. See *Even Shoshan* and Jastrow dictionaries, s.v. niddah.

2. This verse seems to be the bridge phrase, interweaving the two themes, impurity and forbidden sexual relationships.

3. This is derived from the laws of a *zavah* (one who has a discharge), who must wait seven additional days after the discharge stops (Niddah 66a on Lev. 15:23).

4. There is a special dispensation for newlyweds: eleven days instead of twelve. The reason for this is that the loss of blood is probably from the breaking of the hymen and not from the womb. Since one could not know for sure, the rabbis set aside four days plus seven "whites." More logically, if it could be determined within four days that it is extrauterine blood (i.e., from the hymen), then why the seven "whites" altogether? We know from other cases that it is only menstrual blood that made one a niddah; after a Caesarian birth there was no period of separation.

5. This is determined by a series of self-examinations. Staining is considered part of the flow period. In fact, there are more laws on staining than on any other aspect of niddah. Since the laws were so intricate, there were, by acclaim, certain rabbis in each generation who were specialists in the laws of niddah. Questions would be sent to them from great distances. The details were originally spelled out in Mishnah Niddah: finding color or size,

determining whether it is part of the flow or part of seven additional days, where it originates (vagina or womb), the self-examination procedures, whose testimony counts, when are the tests properly done, etc.

6. Since it is not uncommon for a woman to stain for several days after the menstrual flow, this puts an extra burden on couples trying to observe the laws carefully. For women who have long menses (seven or eight days), it means a period of at least two weeks or more of abstention from sex.

7. Although the Bible doesn't describe the purification ritual for niddah (other than the passage of seven days), the rabbis taught that the same procedure used by men applied to women: immersion in living waters (Lev. 15:13).

8. I was never sure about the relevance of that particular prayer. The following, however, seems to suggest itself: niddah and mikveh are the only extant rituals of that period when *tum'ah and taharah* were taken with utmost gravity and when the Temple was the symbol of purity and closeness to God. Moreover, on the day following the immersion, the mendicant would bring two turtledoves to the sanctuary as sacrifice. This additional prayer symbolizes the longing for that time in our past or for messianic redemption of the future.

9. See Rachel Adler, "Tumah and Taharah—Mikveh," in *The First Jewish Catalog,* ed. Richard Siegel, Michael Strassfeld, and Sharon Strassfeld (Philadelphia: The Jewish Publication Society of America, 1973), pp. 167–71.

10. The clearest indication of this was when the Mishnah was codified. Almost two hundred years after the destruction of the Second Temple, the tractate Niddah was classified not in Order Women but in Order Purification. It is also the only one of the twelve mishnayot in Order Purification that has a gemara explicating it.

11. Rashi and Bartenura explain this as rooms, not houses (Niddah 7:2).

12. Several centuries later, segregation was indeed practiced in Babylonia (*Mishneh Torah,* Hilkhot Issurei Bi'ah 11:6, 7, 15).

13. Cf. Samson Raphael Hirsch, *The Pentateuch* (London: I. Levy, 1962), chap. 15.

14. Some contemporary works of one kind or the other are Kalman Kahana, *Daughter of Israel: Laws of Family Purity* (New York: Feldheim, 1970); Norman Lamm, *The Hedge of Roses* (New York: Feldheim, 1968); Pinchas Stolper, *The Road to Responsible Jewish Adulthood* (New York: Union of Orthodox Jewish Congregations of America, 1967); Zev Schostak, *The Purity of the Family: Its Ideology and Its Laws* (New York: Feldheim, 1971).

Jewish Attitudes toward Divorce

TRADITIONAL Jewish divorce law suggests two things: how much change has occurred throughout history and how much more change needs to occur so that the law may serve women non-discriminately.[1] The evolutionary process begins with biblical law:

> A man takes a wife and possesses her. She fails to please him because he finds something obnoxious (*ervat davar*) about her, and he writes her a bill of divorcement, hands it to her, and sends her away from his house. (Deut. 24:1)

Both physical and psychological uprooting were in store for the woman who overly displeased her husband. She had no power to prevent or refuse the divorce, nor was there provision for her to divorce him if she wanted out of the marriage and he didn't. Divorce was the absolute right of the husband, not an illogical consequence of a patriarchal society.

The Bible itself, however, begins the process of modification of these absolute rights. First, the fact that the husband had to write a bill of divorce and present it to his wife served as protection for her (Isa. 50:1; Jer. 3:8). It was a delaying tactic; he could not, in a fit of anger, simply pronounce with finality the formal declaration of divorce. (Irreversible oral divorce was the alternative in ancient Eastern cultures.) Second, a man was required to pay a penalty upon divorce. This is learned from the biblical law of accusation, in which a husband, as grounds for divorce, publicly accuses his wife of premarital sex and of coming to him without her virginity (Deut. 22:13–21). Why would he bother to accuse her publicly, antagonize her family, and humiliate himself in the process when he could have simply divorced her quietly and at will? Because if the charge was upheld, he was released from paying the standard penalty. Third, the Bible describes two instances in which the absolute prohibition against divorce applies: if the husband falsely accused his wife of having had premarital sex; or if a man raped a woman whom he was obligated to marry (providing, of course, she would accept him), he could not thereafter divorce her (Deut. 22:28–29). (This "law of the rapist" may appear crude and rather cruel. In reality, however, it was designed to protect the woman; having lost her virginity through no fault of her own, she would have been otherwise unmarriageable.) Both of these restrictions must be understood in the broader context—the community's prerogative to set limits on a man's absolute, private right of divorce.

The biblical law on divorce comes almost as an aside, as a wrinkle in the law that forbids a man to remarry his ex-wife in the event that she had, in the interim, married another man. This, too, was an encroachment on a man's virtual control over divorce. Moreover, the Bible teaches that there was an alternative to divorce. Polygamy, in a strange sort of way, protected a woman, for a man did not have to divorce one wife in order to take another.

Biblical narrative portrays a different situation altogether. Polygamous marriages were quite rare, yet divorce was also very rare. Women were not driven out wholesale. Even in those isolated instances where a woman was sent away, it was traumatic for the husband as well (Gen. 21:11–12; 1 Sam. 3:14–16). The social sanctions of the community against divorce must have been very strong.

One more word about contexts. Biblical divorce law seems to reflect less an ancient bias of the Hebrew religion concerning women than it does the general Near Eastern male-oriented culture in which biblical law was grounded contextually. Parallel cultures, such as the Sumerian and Hittite, have equivalent divorce rites. The Code of Hammurabi, in force in Mesopotamia during the time of the Patriarchs, records laws on marriage and divorce that are almost identical to biblical law.[2]

Nevertheless, one cannot dismiss biblical divorce law simply as ancient culture-bound mores or sociological axioms of patriarchy.

For Jews, biblical law is revelation and thus the basis of all Halakhah that follows. The rabbis of the Talmud were not insensitive to inequities in biblical divorce law. Little by little, the imbalance was tempered by numerous rabbinic measures that, on the whole, gave women greater protection. Still, the basic principle of man's rights was always there, limiting how far the tradition could go in creating a better distribution of power in family law.

One method by which the rabbis reinforced this principle of absolute right was the selective weighting of scriptural phrases. "And he writes her a bill of divorcement, hands it to her, and sends her away from his house" was interpreted as a sweeping divine principle of the male prerogative. The Mishnah teaches, "The man who divorces is not like the woman who is divorced, because the woman is divorced with her consent or against her will, while the man divorces only with his own free will" (Yevamot 14:1). Only a man can write a bill of divorcement (Gittin 20a; Bava Batra 168a).

On the other hand, the phrase "hands it to her" was not interpreted as divine principle requiring the wife's acceptance or consent; rather, it was explained as procedure. Even as procedure, there was a good deal of leeway: a man may throw the get (bill of divorcement) into her lap or workbasket or date dish or onto the parapet where she might be standing (Gittin 8:1, 77a–79a). Only in some very limited situations is the phrase "hands it to her" used as a principle (Yevamot 113b).

In an early rabbinic dispute between the schools of Hillel and Shammai, a pattern emerges that characterizes much of rabbinic action for centuries to come. Shammai, the strict constructionist of biblical law, maintained that the scriptural words *ervat davar* (Deut. 24:1–4) literally and exclusively meant adultery. Thus, a woman's infidelity was the only legitimate grounds for divorce. (The Catholic church reinforced this strict constructionist view and has wrestled with a most untenable position on divorce ever since.)

Hillel, who generally interpreted the scriptures broadly, understood *ervat davar* as anything offensive to the husband, even burning his food. As in most disputes, rabbinic law followed Hillel (Gittin 9:10).[3]

For the next few centuries, major talmudists reiterated the principle of the unrestricted right of the husband to divorce. The opposing view was not ignored entirely, however. It made itself felt in two ways: in the growing number of halakhic curbs on a man's absolute right and in the moral dicta of the Talmud, such as "he who divorces his wife is hated by God" (Gittin 90b).

Thus, throughout much of rabbinic history, three forces operated in tension: the theory of man's absolute right, the biblical precedents that qualified these rights, and the earliest layer of rabbinic sources that interpreted biblical laws broadly or narrowly. These three constructs could be weighted in every rabbinic decision, depending on one's teacher's views, the climate of the times, or one's inclinations and the particular divorce case at hand.

Rabbinic modification took several forms: increasing the number of cases in which the absolute prohibition against divorce applies, embellishing and encumbering the divorce proceedings, expanding the financial responsibilities of the husband, and enlarging the wife's opportunity to assent or dissent, giving her some mastery over her own fate as a married woman.

1. *Increasing the number of cases.* Two new cases were added beyond the two prohibitions of biblical origin: a man could not divorce a wife who had become insane and thus would have been unable to take care of herself (Yevamot 14:1, 113b), nor could a man divorce a wife who had been taken captive.[4] Another kind of prohibited divorce involved a child bride, not uncommon in oriental Jewish communities.

2. *Embellishing the proceedings.* The complex rules attending actual divorce were spelled out in the Talmud and were further refined in post-talmudic rabbinic literature.[5] These rules apply today just as they did throughout the entire medieval world.

A get must be handwritten by a scribe at the specific instruction of the husband. The language is Aramaic, following the talmudic textual form, with the details of the particular case filled in at the appropriate places. The central part of the get is the husband's declaration: "I will release and set aside you, my wife, in order that you may have authority over yourself to marry any man you desire. . . . You are permitted to every man. . . . This shall be for you a bill of dismissal, a letter of release, a get of freedom" (Gittin 9:1–3; *Mishneh Torah*, Hilkhot Gerushin 4:12).

Great care is taken in the process of writing the get. The scribe has to make a formal gift to the husband of all the writing materials he will use. A get may be declared invalid if the writing, signing, and delivery are misdated. Two male witnesses must sign the get. The husband must present the get to the wife, again in the presence of witnesses (usually the same two men). If this is impossible or impractical, he may appoint an agent of delivery, as may the wife for receipt of the get; the laws concerning agency, however, are even more complicated.

Upon receipt, the wife hands the get over to the bet din (rabbinic court), consisting of three men. They make a tear in the document, signifying the tearing asunder of the relationship as well as the conclusion of the legal transaction of divorce. The bet din files the get for safekeeping and gives a *shtar piturin* (document of release attesting that the wife has received a valid get).

The standard procedures in a divorce are so exact, so detailed, that those in attendance must be experts at it. In many medieval communities, as in modern ones, often there was only one rabbi sufficiently qualified to handle gittin (religious divorce proceedings). The real function of the myriad of laws was to bring the couple into contact with the bet din, whose members understood their role as more than scribes or legal experts. Long before the get was actually drawn, they would try to use their offices to effect a reconciliation. Only after all else failed would they monitor and supervise the final act. This whole process ultimately served to undermine the notion of absolute right. In theory, the husband still had a private and absolute right, but in practice as well as in the popular mind he now had to look to the bet din for sanction.

3. *Expanding the husband's financial responsibilities.* The ketubah (marriage contract) states that the wife is entitled to a return of her dowry and any other properties she had brought with her into the marriage, plus support for her until she remarries. It thus discouraged divorce by levying economic sanctions. If it failed to prevent divorce, however, at least the woman was provided with some measure of security. The ketubah also protected her interests during marriage. The husband was obliged to provide for her according to her station in life, to pay her medical and dental bills, to ransom her if she were taken captive, and to bury her decently

(Ketubbot 4:4–9, 5a; *Mishneh Torah*, Even ha-Ezer, Hilkhot Ishut, 12:2).

The Talmud did not formalize the standard ketubah text but did establish a basic minimum level of recompense. Beyond that, it allowed many variations. Thus, in medieval times, tailor-made ketubot were written where a wife stipulated the conditions under which her husband must grant her a divorce and still pay the ketubah (say, if he took a concubine).

4. *Wife's opportunity to assent or dissent.* In practice, the theoretical right of the husband to put away his wife was eroded continually throughout rabbinic times. Finally, in the eleventh century, Rabbenu Gershom of Mainz formally decreed, by means of a takkanah (rabbinic directive), that a woman could not be divorced without her consent. Woman's will now carried legal force. Although no one would call it by that name, Rabbenu Gershom's decree formally set aside the principle of man's absolute right of divorce.

What the rabbis really were trying to do was protect a woman from being divorced. The end of the tractate on divorce closes with a quote from the prophet Malachi, which summarizes the ethical and moral values that seem to have informed the rabbinic deliberations throughout:

> If a man divorces his first wife, even the altar sheds tears . . . because the Lord has been witness between you and the wife of your youth, against whom you have dealt treacherously, even though she has been your companion and the wife of your covenant. (Gittin 90b)

What about the right of the wife to sue for divorce? The germ of such a notion existed in biblical law, for if a man didn't live up to his contractual obligations, his wife was entitled to bring suit:

> When a man sells his daughter as a slave, . . . if she proves to be displeasing to her master, who designated her for himself, he must let her be redeemed. . . . If he marries another, he must not withhold from this one her food, her clothing, or her conjugal rights. If he fails her in these three ways, she shall go free, without payment. (Exod. 21:7–11)

In other words, this Jewish bondswoman could go out, free of

debts, without a financial settlement but with a bill of divorcement in hand (Mekilta, Mishpatim, sec. 3; Arakhin 5:6; Yevamot 14:1; Gittin 9:8). Because bondswomen probably had very little clout, tradition assumes that the bill of divorcement was mandated by some others with power—the court perhaps, or the city elders (Bava Batra 48a; Yevamot 106a). It was reasonable to assume that if a mere bondswoman was protected by contractual rights, certainly would a wife be who entered the marriage as a free woman.

In rabbinic times the contractual obligations of the husband were expanded and elaborated. Many of the grounds that entitled the wife to divorce reflected great sensitivity to women's needs. Sexual satisfaction, a condition legislated in the Bible, was given real definition by the rabbis. They even legislated the minimum number of times for intercourse, which varied according to the husband's occupation: a sailor had to come ashore at least once every six months, a scholar had to satisfy his wife at least once a week. If a husband refused to meet his wife's conjugal rights, she could exercise her option for divorce through the bet din. If she chose not to exercise this right, her husband could be fined, week by week (Ketubbot 61b–62b).

Impotence also was legitimate grounds for divorce, deriving from an older rabbinic law that actually permitted a woman to make such a charge without bringing proof. A late mishnaic law permitted the husband to contest the accusation but left the burden of proof upon him (Yevamot 65a–b).

If a wife vowed not to have intercourse with her husband and he did not take pains to annul such a vow, she was entitled to sue for divorce (Ketubbot 5:8–9). If she wanted to live in the Holy Land or move from one Palestinian city to Jerusalem and he refused to follow her or to remain there with her (Ketubbot 110b); if he had a serious disease or a continual bad odor from his occupation, like carrying dung or tanning hides (Ketubbot 7:9); if he did not support her in the style to which she had been accustomed or, if he was wealthy, in the style proper for one of his means (Ketubbot 5:8–9); or if he failed to live up to anything in the ketubah, the wife was entitled to sue for divorce. The medieval rabbis added two more grounds for divorce: if he beat her or if he visited prostitutes (*Shulhan Arukh*, Even ha-Ezer, Hilkhot Gittin 154:3, commentary of Rama).[6]

Contractual rights worked as follows: if a husband did not meet his responsibilities to his wife she could go to the bet din, present her case, and obtain a subpoena compelling him to appear to answer the charges. The court would first press him to fulfill his obligations. If he failed to do so, the court could coerce him into granting the divorce by levying economic and social sanctions against him. The law maintained, however, that he was taking this action "of his own free will"; the talmudic phrase is, "We use coercion until he says 'I want to' " (Yevamot 106a). By such legal fiction, the old theory of a man's initiative was retained intact, all the while that, in real life, the woman's rights increased.

A pattern thus emerges. For the husband, the original right to divorce was unchallenged and private, but the historical development of the law served continually to limit it. In the case of the wife, her initial rights were limited, but as Halakhah expanded through the post-biblical generation, these were broadened and formalized. This unmistakable pattern refutes the simple-minded charges that rabbis seized every opportunity to keep women powerless. Quite the reverse is true, considering the rabbinic capacity for interpreting the law, as well as the transfer of male authority from one generation to the next—there is an impressive degree of sensitivity and benevolence in the unfolding of the law. A growing set of obligations of husband to wife and the increasing formalization of her rights to redress through the bet din are clear indications of an attitude of concern toward the woman.

Still, we are left with some large and serious problems. Instead of grappling directly with the sexist principle that only a man had the right to divorce (i.e., write and transfer the get), the rabbis used various legal maneuvers to subvert the original principle. The exclusive right as derived from the Bible was never formally challenged; it was simply chiseled away, bit by bit. As a result, rabbinic authorities in any given generation could revert back to the original notion of a man's power over his wife.

An example of this is found in Rabbenu Gershom's decree that a man could not take more than one wife or divorce his wife against her will (*Shulhan Arukh*, Even ha-Ezer 1:10, 119:6, Rama). This was a significant breakthrough. But a minor qualification was appended to the end of this takkanah: if a recalcitrant wife refused a divorce or was physically unable to accept, a husband could deposit the get with the rabbinic court, announce his intention to divorce, receive the approval of a hundred rabbis, and then would be free to take another wife. Thus here, as in other instances, the more egalitarian decision concerning a woman's right of consent could be reversed or tempered in certain situations on the theory that the husband's legal right could not be abrogated. Somehow, in special-need cases, the Halakhah managed to find a way round the biblical and talmudic requirement that the husband hand her a get. One need not wonder why the Halakhah did not find a parallel—and equally necessary—loophole to allow a wife release from a similar situation.

This brings us to the second and more formidable problem: a woman could not and can not present her husband with a get and thereby divorce him, although she can do the actual writing of it. The theory is that the husband is the one who created the bond and therefore he must be the one to sever it (Kiddushin 56: 9b). Nor is there any provision in Jewish law by which a get is granted judicially in the absence of or without the consent of the husband. Only the husband can grant a get.

This can give rise to the agunah, the anchored wife, anchored to an absentee husband.[7] There are two types of agunot: a woman whose husband either has deserted, is insane, or is missing and presumed dead but whose death has not been verified by two witnesses; and a woman who is the wife of a recalcitrant husband who refuses the get for ignoble reasons. This latter type of agunah points up the potential for real abuse in Jewish divorce law. Indeed, in every generation there have been sinister tales of spite, blackmail, extortion, and delay until the wife has met her recalcitrant husband's price.

Throughout the centuries rabbis have tried continually to alleviate the plight of the agunah. In talmudic times the bet din accepted her own testimony as sufficient proof of the husband's death, a sharp reversal of Halakhah, which required two male witnesses in all matters that come before the rabbinic courts; this is to protect her from the possibility that she might become forever anchored to an absentee husband (Gittin 3a). In talmudic law, a man was not permitted to leave the community without guaranteeing an agreement to divorce if he did not plan to return within a specified time (Gittin 6:5, 6; Ketubbot 11b). This was a regular feature of medieval Jewish society, where husbands had to leave for extended periods of time in order to earn a livelihood.[8]

In this era, contemporary rabbis expended great effort to release the agunot of the Holocaust. The Israeli rabbinate, too, has adapted Halakhah to Israel's current precarious reality. In a broad move, it required all married male soldiers to deposit a conditional writ of divorce with the bet din before going to the front lines. This was based on ancient precedent (Ketubbot 9b). Moreover, after the Yom Kippur War, in a single religious enactment, over a thousand young women were released from what otherwise would have been extended agunah proceedings.

Still, there remain many cases of agunot in Jewish communities around the world. Some cases are too hard to crack, some take years to settle, some women find they must pursue and beg. Despite the compassion of the many rabbis who resolve individual cases, women testify to a certain humiliating quality inherent in the basic notion of agunah, in her status in the community, and in the very process of release from this state.

Ironically, an open society has worked to the disadvantage of the Jewish woman who wants to bring suit for divorce. In the closed, relatively autonomous Jewish communities of the past, religious authorities could level sanctions against a recalcitrant husband; in modern societies, however, the rabbinic courts (outside of Israel) have authority only over those people who voluntarily submit themselves to its dictates. Contemporary batei din, trying to function in a secular society, have a low rate of success in their power of subpoena. Even in Israel there are men who have chosen to remain in jails to which the bet din remanded them rather than free their wives with a get.

Thus, in the attempt to reduce the disparity between man's power and woman's powerlessness in divorce, the rabbis tried hard—perhaps not hard enough. It would have taken little more collective responsibility to close the gap altogether, to create a situation of real equality under the law. The rabbis assumed wide powers of interpretation of divine law, and even of innovation, in situations where the general needs of the community called for accommodation to reality rather than rationalization of an unwieldy status quo. That the rabbis did not go the final step in equalizing divorce law indicates that they were guided in their interpretations by principles of paternalism and hierarchy rather than of equality of male and female. For this they cannot be faulted, given the almost universal nature of the sexual hierarchy. Failure of some contemporary rabbis, however, to use precedents that do exist and failure to acknowledge that past improvements in divorce law are but part of a continuing process leads one to conclude that many of them prefer to maintain the principle of absolute right, apologetic platitudes notwithstanding.

Several solutions have been formulated in modern times. Reform Judaism understood the Halakhah to be indefensible in terms of the ethical and social categories central to Reform, so it simply dropped gittin and said civil divorce will do. If one is concerned more for equality than for tradition, that solution meets the test. If, however, one's commitment is to both more equality and greater Jewish observance in every sphere of life, then that is no solution at all. In fairness, it should be added that Reform is asking of itself different questions today; it is searching for ways to make Jewish law altogether more encompassing. The time seems ripe for Reform to rethink its stance on gittin. Meanwhile, it has no operative Jewish divorce law.

Reconstructionism has formulated a solution that lies somewhere between the two ends of the spectrum—or, more correctly, at the two ends of the spectrum. The Reconstructionist rabbinate uses the traditional get and all of the attendant procedures. When a previously divorced woman wants to remarry but has been unable to secure a get from her former husband, the Reconstructionist bet din simply will give her a *shtar piturin*, a document that declares her free to remarry, even though she has no get, nor has her marriage been annulled.

For the last three decades, Conservative Judaism has gone through three stages of emendation in an attempt to eliminate potential abuse yet remain faithful to inherited tradition.[9] These changes are instructive, for they give some idea of the possibilities, the problems, and the processes involved.

The Lieberman ketubah was used first in 1954. By means of a takkanah, Rabbi Saul Lieberman appended a t'nai (conditional clause) to the standard ketubah: if the marriage ends in civil divorce, either party may invoke the authority of the bet din to determine the Jewish course of action, the transfer of a get. If either party refuses the get, he or she becomes liable to suit in civil court. Presumably the court will enforce the bet din's decision. Although this ketubah generally is no longer used for the purposes of resolving cases of a recalcitrant spouse, it is used widely in marriages performed by Conservative rabbis. (One of the problems with this ketubah was that it didn't cover divorce cases where the ketubah had not been used originally. Moreover, the credibility of its threat depended on its enforceability in a civil court, and this remains in doubt. The Lieberman clause was rejected by the Orthodox as being halakhically invalid because of its indeterminate nature. First, the damages [knas, fine] were not spelled out and, therefore, one would not sign such a contract making oneself liable to an undetermined penalty. The Lieberman ketubah, however, does use the word pitzuim, damages, a term often employed in contracts and one that is halakhically valid; this is about as specific as one would want to be at the time of a marriage ceremony. Second, the pledge the groom was making was considered an asmakhta—a pledge to pay a fine for a situation that he was not really expecting would come to pass.)

The second stage was adoption of the Berkovits t'nai in 1968, which differs from the Lieberman solution in that it attached conditions to the act of marriage itself. Rabbi Eliezer Berkovits based his work on two elements: the principle that a marriage could be nullified by the rabbinic authorities, and the precedent in Jewish law of establishing specific conditions for a marriage. Unmet, such conditions would enable a bet din to determine that the marriage was voided retroactively and never legally constituted. This precedent had also been used by the rabbis of Paris in the late nineteenth century. The Berkovits conditions were that the couple not be separated for an undue amount of time, that neither refuses (or becomes unable) to give or accept a divorce, and that the wife does not conceive out of adulterous union. The Conservative law committee modified this, and Rabbi Edward Gershfield worked out a text to this effect: if our marriage should end in a civil divorce and within six months thereafter I give you a get, our marriage will remain valid and binding; if, however, six months have passed and I do not give you a get, then our marriage will have been null and void. This was not appended to the ketubah; it was signed as a separate pre-nuptial agreement. In this instance there was no need to turn to the civil courts to enforce the get. On the other hand, its being a separate document was also its weakness; couples were reluctant to sign it at such a happy moment in their lives. (This proposal was rejected by the Orthodox on the grounds that marriage is an unconditional commitment and conditional marriages and divorces thereby are rendered invalid by consummation of the marriage.[10])

The third-stage solution, widely operative in Conservative Judaism today in problem divorce cases, is a broader application of *havka'at kiddushin* (the power of the rabbis to annul marriages ab initio) (Bava Batra 48b; Gittin 33a; Kiddushin 3a). It is based on the talmudic principle that all who marry within the Jewish community do so with the implied consent of and under the conditions laid down by the rabbis. (The phrase "according to the laws of Moses and Israel" is in the ketubah and is also a central part of the ring ceremony.) Thus, a man's act of marrying a woman is validated by the rabbis' sanction of that act. Just as they give sanction, so can they remove sanction; the marriage continues to exist only as long as the rabbis agree to its existence. If the rabbis remove their sanction because of certain conditions no longer operating, the original act of kiddushin (betrothal) is voided. Retroactively, it becomes simply an act of giving a gift, such as a ring. And what about a marriage that was consummated? Even there, the rabbis could declare the sexual liaison to have been a non-marital act (i.e., an act of prostitution).

How does it work today in Conservative Judaism? In the case of a recalcitrant husband, the wife first goes to her own rabbi for help. If he cannot compel the husband (ex-husband by civil law) to grant a get, the wife then appears before a special bet din established by the Conservative rabbinate. She produces her civil divorce as well as proof of previous good-faith attempts to secure a get. If the bet din is satisfied, it will issue a document retroactively declaring the marriage null and void, and she is then free to remarry. This differs from the Berkovits t'nai in that no additional conditions are attached to the marriage and no special agreement needs to be signed. This, too, was rejected by many Orthodox rabbis, on the grounds that the power to annul marriages was used only in limited instances and in post-talmudic times the power to annul marriages has been constricted.

What has been done by the Orthodox community? Beyond rejecting the strides taken by Conservative Judaism there has been little movement. Meanwhile, increasing numbers of traditional women who have sued for divorce face the threat of blackmail for a get.

The winds of change are in the air, however. In 1967, when Berkovits published his book, T'nai be-nisuin u-ve-get (Conditional clause in marriage and divorce agreements), he intended it not for Conservative Judaism but for the Orthodox community of which he is a member. Initially he had the approval of his teacher, the eminent posek Harav Yechiel Yaakov Weinberg. With increasing pressure from the right, the ailing Weinberg withdrew his approval, and the vocal elements in the Orthodox rabbinate utterly rejected Berkovits's proposal. There was quiet support for Berkovits, but quiet support doesn't help much.

In the early 1970s, Ze'ev Falk, an Orthodox professor at the Hebrew University, updated the facts.[11] He gave a generous survey of all previous solutions offered, stating that the recalcitrant husband situation is more widespread in Israel than in the United States, with cases often taking up to ten years to resolve through the religious courts, ten years during which a woman cannot remarry. In 1977, Irwin S. Haut[12] traced the history of an ancient takkanah enacted by the geonim and used by them for over three hundred years: if, after twelve months, the wife does not relent in her pursuit of a get, the husband can be forced by the bet din to give one to her. This takkanah was enacted long ago to put an end to the practice of Jewish women hiring gentile strong-arm men "to force him until he says I want to." Haut calls for the Israeli rabbinate, as a centralized authority, to enact a new takkanah, along the lines of the geonic one that long since has expired. It would compel a man who lives outside Israel and who has been granted a civil divorce to give his wife a get; if a man so enjoined by the bet din, whether in the diaspora or in Israel, still refuses, then the bet din shall declare the marriage annulled or dissolved. The difference between this solution and the Conservative one today is the use of a takkanah and the centralization of authority in the Israeli rabbinate.

In *Jewish Women in Jewish Law*, widely read in Orthodox circles, Moshe Meiselman acknowledges the problem of recalcitrant husbands.[13] In his unswerving desire not to touch the halakhic status quo, he calls on the secular courts for a solution: the civil court should enforce the decision of the bet din when it recommends a get and none is forthcoming. Meiselman doesn't deal with the First Amendment issue; moreover, although he acknowledges the very sporadic success in civil courts thus far, he waves that problem aside with the unfounded optimism that the problems will be solved by better education of civil judges.[14] But he does call for repair.

At its annual convention in 1978, the Rabbinical Council of America devoted a major session to the contemporary problems in gittin. Rabbi Meir Feldblum, a noted halakhic authority, raised the issues and several solutions. At Bar Ilan University's Conference on Jewish Women in 1978, the president, Rabbi Emanuel Rackman, an acknowledged leader of modern Orthodoxy, opened the deliberations with a halakhic history of *havka'at kiddushin*. He forthrightly called for its use by the rabbinate. Several months later he repeated this call in print; his message was picked up on the front page of several American Jewish weeklies.

Finally, there have been the efforts of women, in smaller and larger communities. A group of Orthodox women in a Canadian city simply announced that none of them would go to the mikveh until a friend of theirs received a free get from her ex-husband, who was holding out for twenty-five thousand dollars. The woman received her get in no time. In 1980, an organization called G.E.T. was formed by traditional women who intend to apply pressure until women Get Equal Treatment in Jewish divorce proceedings.

Nevertheless, the problems of inequity remain, with an increasing number of women—the traditional women—paying a steep price for their adherence to Halakhah. What is more, an altogether new problem exists, unprecedented in Jewish history: a community operating by four different sets of divorce law, as if we were four different communities.

What remains to be done, then, is to formulate a solution that would solve both problems: eliminate any potential for abuse of women and unite all branches of Judaism in its universal acceptance. To achieve both means that all Jews will have to accept that there is something distinctive about being a Jew and living under Jewish law. It means that we will all have a heightened sense of awareness that marriage and divorce and every other sweep of our lives should be experienced properly within the framework of a holy community.

Like most of our rituals, divinely mandated and contoured by several millennia of Jewish living, a Jewish divorce is about as finely tuned to the human need of the moment as one could anticipate. Unlike the final moment in a civil divorce, a Jewish divorce is not an adversary situation. There is no litigation, no grounds, no recriminations, no attempts at reconciliation, no high drama. In fact, there is almost no conversation. All of that, whatever there was of it, took place at another time. The divorce itself is an unadorned legal procedure, performed at the last stage, an act that lends a profound sense of finality and closure to the relationship. This is no small feat, for as social scientists increasingly report, a sense of closure is one of the most difficult stages for one to reach in the throes of a divorce.

But it is not its worthiness as a therapeutic tool on which the strength of Jewish divorce rests. A Jewish divorce, like a Jewish marriage, a Jewish birth, or a Jewish death, is, quite simply, the way a Jew lives. This is how Jews have done these things for several millennia; this is the manner in which one marks oneself as a Jew today.

Thus leaders of all of the branches of Judaism will have to come together and talk to each other in order to work out a mutually acceptable solution, each recognizing the other as part of *klal Yisrael*, the total Jewish community. Smug, isolationist positions will have to fall away.

To help that process along, women will have to increase their efforts. Given the current nature of entrenched interests and institutional hard lines, Jewish women of every political and religious shade must attempt to bring together the dissonant ends and to fill the vacuum created by loss of initiative of current religious leaders. Who can know the impact of a thousand women protesting to the leaders of Reform Judaism for restoration of a halakhic Jewish divorce law? Who can know the effect of a thousand Jews calling on the bet din of the Rabbinical Council of America to reexamine the current injustices in halakhic divorce? (Surely the rabbinic authorities would approach their storehouse of halakhic precedents and principles with a different sense of urgency, in much the same way they have done in so many individual cases of agunot.) Who knows but that the pressure on Conservative leadership will spur them to seek greater cooperation with all strata of the Jewish religious community?

It is hard to project what the optimal form of revision ultimately will be. Perhaps it will be along the lines of *havka'at kiddushin*, used by the Conservative bet din and recommended by numerous Orthodox scholars. Perhaps it will be a conditional clause added to the ketubah. Perhaps the diaspora rabbinate will place it in the hands of the Israeli rabbinate, where the centralization of authority in family law lends itself more easily to global rather than individual solutions.

Perhaps, with a new sense of equality of women, the revision will take the form of a takkanah that will empower a woman to transfer a get. If, as halakhists defensively point out, marriage is a change of status rather than unilateral acquisition of woman by man, if a woman is a mutually active and reciprocal partner in all of these transactions, if divorce is a more halakhically correct way of ending a marriage than annulment, then having a woman deliver the get where a man refuses, may be a better halakhic solution all around. A usable precedent may be one that circumvents the law requiring a husband to pay for the writing of the get. When a man refused to pay the scribal fee, the court required the woman to pay so that the husband would not cause her delay in securing her freedom (Bava Batra 168a).

All of this brings us to the question of tradition and change. In view of the fact that the unfolding Halakhah on divorce reflects an unmistakable pattern of limiting the husband's and expanding the wife's rights, the rabbis of today no longer can say they can not "work it out." To say their hands are tied, or to say they can resolve an individual problem but not find a global solution, is to deny their collective responsibility. Worse, it bespeaks a lack of rabbinic will to find a halakhic way. What they are really saying is they are not worthy of the authority vested in them, for well they know that the only person whose hands are tied is the woman whose family must pay blackmail.

If there were no abuses in the area of divorce, I would not mind the male prerogative preserved and this law untouched. A one-sided kiddushin harbors no real injustice and ought to be appreciated for what it is: an ancient rabbinic tradition, the Jewish way men and women have married for thousands of years. In that alone there is great value and sentiment.

But given the opposite condition today—increasing abuse— halakhists ought to commit themselves not only to alleviation of individual distress here and there but to the notion of a just law. For alleviation of an individual is not justice for an entire system. If halakhists do not put their minds and energies to this problem, then I suspect that we will see what we have seen in the past—the regulation of one more area of human relations shrinking in the hands of the interpreters of Jewish law, as growing numbers of Jews solve their problems elsewhere.[15]

Broad-scale resolution of the inequity would serve another advantage. It would eliminate the enormous cost in rabbinic time and energy now spent in trying to procure a get from a recalcitrant husband. Religious leaders would then be free to attend to the real problem: the factors behind the rising rate of divorce, the unreal expectations of marriage, the ideology of "me first," the impatience men and women have when it comes to working steadily at a relationship.

Some years ago, when I first began to research the subject, I felt a great ambivalence, even a sense of dread, as I spoke of fundamental change of the biblical principle of absolute right. Part of that dread grows out of my spiritual rootedness in a community that, at most, allows itself to speak in hushed tones about gradual changes over a period of two millennia. Nor am I unmindful of the

fact that the divinity of the Torah has remained so strong throughout the ages, precisely because the rabbis were so careful not to
forbid what was permitted and permit what was forbidden. By
nature and education, then, I have always preferred solutions that
involved least change in the basic structure of Halakhah.

Nevertheless, I must stop and ask whether half-way steps would
be doing a disservice to Jewish women, say, ten generations from
now. Has that not happened to women in this generation of Jewish living in an open society? Moreover, with increased understanding of law and process I must question whether the principle
is truly principle. Perhaps the essence of biblical law is the delivery of the get, a formal document that gives proper legal and
psychological closure to a relationship. Perhaps the male prerogative—man giving the get to woman—is but form and not essence.
Perhaps it was an accident of history that a pervasive notion of
hierarchy of the sexes enabled procedure to be hardened into principle, thereby blocking out other more important principles such as
tikkun olam, improvement of the social order, equality for all members of the covenanted community.

Inevitably, there will always be injustice and imbalances in
every divorce situation; that, sadly, is the nature of the dissolution
of a human relationship. But the law should not discriminate
against one sex. And if there is one woman in each generation who
suffers unnecessarily as a result of the law, then the law is biased
against all women.

If, as I believe, Judaism is the most ethical, most sensitive of all
religions, if since revelation Judaism has moved toward its own
best values, a reinterpretation that would bring about greater
equality should be articulated not in categories of change/no change
but rather as part of the organic growth of a holy people as it
moves through history.

NOTES

1. I recommend four excellent sources on this topic, two in English and
two in Hebrew: David Werner Amram, *The Jewish Law of Divorce in the
Bible and Talmud* (New York: Hermon, 1968); Ze'ev Falk, *Divorce Action by*

the Wife in the Middle Ages (Jerusalem: Hebrew University, 1973); Benzion Schereschewsky, *Dinei mishpahah* [Family law] (Jerusalem: R. Mass, 1967); Eliezer Berkovits, *T'nai be-nisuin u-ve-get* [Conditional clause in the marriage and divorce agreements] (Jerusalem: Mossad Harav Kuk, 1967).

2. See James B. Pritchard, ed., *Ancient Near Eastern Texts* (Princeton: Princeton University Press, 1969), pp. 137–40; Roland de Vaux, *Ancient Israel: Its Life and Institutions* (New York: McGraw-Hill, 1965), ch. 2.

3. Rabbi Akiba extended this further: it was within the rights of the husband to discard his wife if he found another he liked better; he based his interpretation on the phrase "if she found no favor in his eyes." See Meyer S. Feldblum, *Talmudic Law and Literature* (New York: Yeshiva University, 1969), pp. 221–3.

4. Since this was an abrogation of the biblical right of the husband, the rabbis saw fit to explain their action. They forbade it because they understood the consequences, that the woman would become destitute and helpless and an easy prey. But they "covered" their humane tracks with a legal rationale. Since the Torah required the get be given "into her hand," it must have been meant that she be capable of receiving it (i.e., in possession of her full faculties; this was one instance where "into her hand" was applied as principle and not merely as procedure). Further, the Torah described a divorcée as "one who is cast away from his house and, therefore, will not return. But an insane person, you send her away and she keeps coming back" (Yevamot 113b). This is an example of that profound rabbinic process, of making rabbinic law "continuous" with the Torah. Interestingly, when Maimonides describes this ruling, he cites only the humane reason and not the legally continuous one (*Mishneh Torah*, Hilkhot Gerushin 10:23). Tracing the process a step further, in medieval times, after the ban on polygamy was enacted, the rabbis occasionally granted dispensation to the husband of an insane woman to take another wife. This was permitted, however, only when the insanity was deemed incurable and the husband provided adequately for her care, a rather humane solution all around. Maimonides' formulation is a bit harsher: the husband sets her aside, takes another wife, and when she becomes well he then divorces her. In other words, there is no condition of incurability here. Moreover, the husband is not required to provide shelter, medical care, nor ransom money (*Mishneh Torah*, Hilkhot Gerushin 10:23). Obviously, Maimonides applied neither Rabbenu Gershom's ban against forcible divorce nor exceptions to it. On the other hand, Maimonides went further than Rabbenu Gershom in certain respects.

5. The *Shulhan Arukh* lists 101 steps in the rules of procedure attending divorce. The Rama adds several notes and refinements to that list. See Amram, *Jewish Law of Divorce*, pp. 192–204. Another work used by those who deal regularly with gittin is the *Kav Naki*, the seventeenth-century comprehensive manual of divorce procedures.

6. There was even a Spanish tradition that required no grounds at all: "If she says, 'I despise him,' in my opinion we compel him to divorce her immediately, for she isn't like a captive that she must have intercourse with someone who is hateful to her" (*Mishneh Torah*, Hilkhot Ishut 14:8).

7. See Chaim Grade's novel, *The Agunah* (Boston: Twayne, 1974).

8. See Israel Abrahams, *Jewish Life in the Middle Ages* (New York: Atheneum, 1969), p. 90.

9. See Seymour Siegel, "The Living Halakhah: Conservative Judaism and Jewish Law," *United Synagogue Review* (Winter 1979).

10. See Moshe Meiselman, *Jewish Women and Jewish Law* (New York: Ktav, 1978), pp. 103–8.

11. Ze'ev Falk, *The Divorce Action by the Wife in Jewish Law* (Jerusalem: ILRCL, 1973).

12. Irwin H. Haut, "A Problem in Jewish Divorce Law: An Analysis and Some Suggestions," *Tradition* 16 (Spring 1977): 29–49.

13. Meiselman, *Jewish Women*, ch. 14.

14. Several scholars and legal historians have shown the inherent fallacy of relying on the civil courts in this matter. See, for example, A. Leo Levin and Mayer Kramer, *New Provisions in the Ketubah: A Legal Opinion* (New York: Yeshiva University, 1955).

15. See Stephen Beiner, "Israeli Divorce Proceedings: A Comparative Study" (unpublished).

The Issue of Abortion

I TENSE at the thought of getting caught up in the controversy over abortion. Emotionally, theologically, as a Jew, and most of all as a mother who is nurtured daily by the sights and sounds of her children, I am opposed to abortion. And yet, the other facets of unwanted pregnancy cannot be ignored—fatigued and harassed parents, the shame of rape, the premature end of youth (in the case of teenage pregnancy), the degradation and danger of coat-hanger abortions, and, not least, the overwhelming and exclusive claim a child makes on a woman's life for many of her strongest years. I therefore have supported legalized abortion reform, with the full knowledge of the ambivalence of my position.

Social issues, whatever their nature, are rarely clear-cut, with all the truth on one side. This is particularly so in the case of abortion. Here we find conflicts between the generally accepted halakhic position on abortion and the individual needs of women. There is also the disjunction between concern for world overpopulation and concern for Jewish survival, where sheer numbers are significant. There is the disparity between the opportunity to increase medical knowledge and the excesses of fetal experimentation. Finally, there is conflict in the confusion of options, as well as in areas of control assigned to religion or state or individual. What changes, one must ask, does a society undergo when ever greater areas of morality become matters of individual conscience?

But one is forced to make choices, and because all life decisions are made with competing claims in mind, I must, however tenuously, come down on the side of abortion as a legal option in the

United States. Moreover, as a member of a faith community that has a stake in the laws of this country, I believe that we ought to reexamine the Jewish tradition to see where the more lenient interpretation of the Jewish law can support legalized abortion. We should do this, however, with reservations, and also with a sense of urgency, in order to inform our people and society at large with our own value system.

All of this means exploring new roles and responsibilities for the halakhic community rather than continuing to expend time and energy, as is now the case, in trying to impose the stricter interpretation of Jewish law upon a nation that to a large degree has moved in the other direction. To permit abortion as a medical option, yet to educate and infuse society with a transcendent perspective, may be the greatest contribution that moral and religious communities can make. It ultimately may end the long, grisly history of illegal abortions yet simultaneously begin to curb facile abortions. It also may help a searching society to internalize an ethic that incorporates a sense of the preciousness of human relationships and of life itself.

The antiabortion elements in the Jewish community commonly cite the following arguments to support their claims:

1. The dangers to which legalized abortions could lead, that is, abuses of scientific manipulation, such as eugenics or euthanasia.
2. The halakhic view opposing abortion except in lifesaving cases.
3. The devaluation of human life in the abortion process itself—men and women taking matters into their own hands, "transcending their role as humans and undertaking to play God."[1]

Regarding the first argument, there is no evidence that legalizing abortion necessarily will lead to greater abuses. Sweden liberalized its abortion laws many years ago, yet Germany, without a long history of legalized abortion, conceived of and executed the Aryan master race plan and the Mengele medical experiments. This domino argument is not relevant to the abortion controversy. In good measure, the responsibility of the halakhic community is not to say that abortion will lead to abuse, but rather ever to be alert that it does not.

As for the halakhic position on abortion, in reviewing the literature it appears that there are a number of different views, some lenient, others strict.[2] These all derive from several basic sources in the Torah, Mishnah, and Talmud. The most direct statement on the matter is to be found in Mishnah Oholoth 7:6: "If a woman is having a hard labor, and her life is in danger, then the fetus may be cut up and extracted limb by limb, for her life takes precedence over that of the fetus. But if the greater part of the fetus has already been born, one may not touch it, for the life of one person may not be taken for that of another." Until its birth, then, the fetus is not a *nefesh*, a human life.

Halakhah does not view abortion as murder, as a crime calling for capital punishment. Nor does it ascribe rights to the fetus, which explains the relative absence of the "right-to-life" stance in the Jewish antiabortion campaign. The Torah teaches that if a man strikes a pregnant woman and kills the fetus, he is fined only damages for property (Exod. 21:12, 22–23); ironically, this fine is paid to the husband, as if the fetus were considered his property.

Around these central themes there has arisen a whole body of rabbinic literature dealing with such questions as the status of the fetus before and after forty days—the Talmud describes the fetus as "water" until the fortieth day—and what constitutes legitimate circumstances for abortion (Yevamot 69b; Niddah 15b, 30a–b; Berakhot 60a).

On the whole, the traditional Jewish view on abortion has been more permissive than the classic Christian view. Yet even where abortion was permitted by halakhists, it was performed only in cases of therapeutic abortions where not to abort would constitute a grave threat to the life or health of the mother. With very few exceptions, the health of the fetus is not seen as a valid reason for abortion. Thus, in those minority opinions that permit abortion for malformed fetuses, such as in the Thalidomide cases, the rabbinic decisions are based on a broad interpretation of the threat to the mother's health and not on considerations of the potential suffering of the child.[3]

The real issue we face today, however, is not therapeutic abortion but abortion on demand. In this regard there are very few Jewish responsa dealing with abortion based on personal, economic, or family-planning considerations. This can be understood historically. In the life of the traditional Jewish communities in premodern times, where even birth control was restricted carefully and where the procreative function was high on the list of mitzvot, new life was valued, particularly so because life altogether was precarious: you had to have eight children if you wanted four to survive. And until modern times, abortion was not common in the general culture (Jews in the diaspora always have been affected by the mores of the prevailing society). Furthermore, in our own day, when many Jews opt to have only one or two children, and when the issue of abortion has assumed national importance, most Jews do not look to rabbinic guidance for decisions in these areas.

Since there are no traditional Jewish precedents for abortion on demand, one way to maintain some integrity within the halakhic framework could be to broaden the interpretation of therapeutic abortion, to extend the principle of precedence of the mother's actual life and health to include serious regard for the quality of life as well. By linking one to the other—respect for the quality of her life to the ancient halakhic regard for her life when the embryo threatens her physically—this would help the decision-makers more readily to adjust between legitimate and illegitimate need. Indeed, in the halakhic literature there exist several precedents of exactly that nature. In the nineteenth and twentieth centuries there have been responsa permitting abortion in cases of rape of a married woman, in cases where the birth would cause extended suffering to the mother, or, as noted above, in the minority decisions on malformed fetuses. These decisions were made by respected halakhists who moved in their application of the law from purely physical to mental and emotional considerations of the mother—which is what the current issue regarding abortion is all about.[4]

Although one can envision a halakhic stance that urges avoidance of abortion for all the familiar traditional and theological reasons, the circumstances under which abortion is permissible may be widened. Such conditions may include the emotional inability to cope with childbearing and rearing—for example, the need to support oneself (or one's spouse) through school, the time required for a marriage to stabilize, overwhelming responsibilities to other children, and so forth. In these cases, abortion should be seen as a necessity rather than an evil. Indeed, many mitzvot are interdependent functions of timing and of the conditions they regulate.

Returning to the third traditional argument against abortion—the devaluation of human life and the dehumanizing effect of abortion upon individuals and society—I find merit in the view that the problem with easy abortion is that it may become simply a means of birth control, devoid of the seriousness regarding the mystery of human conception. I understood this when I read, some years ago, of the strike of nurses in a large East Coast hospital. They could no longer abide the continual sight of aborted fetuses piled high in the bins of the abortion theater. The image that followed in my mind was the heaps of corpses that numbed the Allied inspection teams in Auschwitz, 1945, and that numb the Jewish people forever. It is the ultimate desecration of man and woman made in the image of God. Here, truly, is the dialectic in the abortion issue with which one must come to grips.

The question then arises: how can one retain the principles of reverence for life built into the Halakhah while broadening the grounds for abortion.

One answer is that sanctions for abortion—or against it—should be framed as part of a theological whole, in which conception and birth are core segments of that theology. A Jew should ask and answer personal questions with wider reference to a religious code that has as its value-source God and community. This is the reverse of how abortion decisions often are made today.

It will take courage for the framers of Jewish law to rule that in certain instances abortion is the higher morality, in keeping with overall principles of *kavod ha-briot* (respect for all living things) and *tzelem elohim* ("in the image of God")—principles that sometimes are lost in the myriad of laws developed to express those very priorities. For example, Jewish law, as we have seen, sanctions abortion in cases where the mother's health is at stake. In various responsa, rabbinic authorities have extended this notion to include her psychological health as well.[5] Those responsa could support new ones, which would encompass such variables as physical strength, stress, even delay in child rearing for purposes of family planning. Further, the fact that in Jewish law love and marriage are positive values should allow room to deal with cases where a wife becomes pregnant before the couple has had a chance to develop a solid relationship.

The principle of ve-hai ba-hem ("and you shall live by them," the mitzvot, that is [Lev. 18:5])[6] could be applied to the abortion of a Tay-Sachs or deformed fetus. Here the dignity of tzelem elohim must be interpreted not as opposing abortion lest it lead to dehumanization but rather in the light of the suffering and the inevitable death that will ensue. It is true that some children with deformities are more loved and evoke deeper feelings of compassion than do perfect specimens. Yet institutions are full of pathetic, rejected, malformed, non-functioning children who eke out a miserable, inhuman life and whose parents have deep wells of guilt. In this situation, forced birth is the dehumanizing situation. Finally, the fact that the Talmud considered a fetus as water until the fortieth day allows further room for abortion under wider circumstances.

Halakhists should not be fearful of extending Jewish law to create a better meshing of personal needs with traditional dictates. This does not mean that the Halakhah must legitimate itself by simply saying yes to all its claimants. It does mean that in moving toward a more realistic position, its negative value-judgments also will be taken seriously. By moving in these directions, we will not be compromising the Halakhah. The rabbis took the goals and ideals of the Torah as their starting points and showed how to strive for the ideal in a real life with all its conflicting claims. By opening its stance on abortion, traditional Judaism could go on to develop new roles and responsibilities for itself today.

One such responsibility could be to support research on earlier and self-implemented methods of pregnancy detection. If modern science has been able to develop the pill (which is halakhically permissible despite the fact that it circumvents the goal of procreation), then it is presumably capable also of developing the morning-after detection and antidote kit. It goes without saying that the halakhic community should investigate and develop better methods of contraception and wider education on birth control.

Some additional responsibilities could be the establishment of adoption agencies, continued vigilance and monitoring of the effects of legal abortion to prevent abuses, greater communal sharing of responsibility in raising and educating children, better sex education, and more mature responsibility for one's sex life.

The halakhic stance must not become simply a matter of opposition to abortion, with grudging exceptions granted in particular cases. Rather, the emphasis should be that alternatives to abortion are available, but that reasons for having children are far more compelling. To wit: every child, who is special and unique, has the right to a life of love and care. Children also return love and care; they are precious and not creatures who get in the way. In these parlous times, when children often are regarded as nuisances or hindrances to self-fulfillment, these basic truths ought to be stressed.

A Jewish theology of abortion should postulate that the Jewish people need to increase their birth rate and replenish themselves after Auschwitz, even as we seriously attend to the general question of world overpopulation; what is good for the rest of the world is not always good for the Jews. Although one does not have a child for the sake of history, many Jews of this generation have understood instinctively that creating life is the only real response one can make after death.[7] These ideas cannot be coerced; rather, they must be set forth as valid and desirable options, competing in a society where the opposite messages are currently more popular.

What effect would all this have upon the Halakhah itself? It well may lead to an extension of the halakhic ambits, from a stress on proper observance of rituals to a stress on proper ethical, social, and sexual decision making. As Jews we have always believed in an ethical, judicial system that governs every aspect of life. There is a great need today to reinstate that capacity in areas of ethics and morality. This may encourage more Jews—even those who consider themselves observant of Jewish law—to take the Halakhah seriously as a moral force in their lives.

Abortion is really a symptom of a larger problem. Ours is a society that establishes the value of goods over relationships, possessions over people, ease and comfort over labor and giving. As creatures of modernism, we tend to see our daily existence as of cosmic importance while losing sight of our real consequence in the course of human civilization. We try to hide these truths of human existence with pills, material goods, diversions of every sort. Even sexual ecstasy becomes a cover for real relationships. The imbalance in our society is too obvious to miss. As a result, contemporary society borders on the selfish. And Jews are no better than any other group in this respect.

The present clamor for abortion is, in part, an overreaction to the past, to the way women feel about their roles in society, their constriction of options other than motherhood, their dependency, their powerlessness. The ultimate expression of this feeling is the notion that many feminists have made central to their claims for abortion—the right to control their own bodies. This, to my mind, is too narrow a focus when considering the miracle of life creation. Furthermore, such an attitude releases men from their responsibility, thereby reinforcing the sexist models that it seeks to undermine. Moral theologians ought to attend to the climate of disabilities and inequities regarding women—in the larger society and in the Jewish community—so that the situation will not foment into a final crisis, with rejection of childbirth and child rearing as the expressions of dissatisfaction.

Hand in hand with the greater halakhic responsibility and flexibility regarding abortion should be also a critique of the society that currently reduces human concerns to such issues. Along with this must come some moral guidance on how a whole society can begin to integrate those values that have at their center reverence for life itself.

NOTES

1. Rabbinical Council of America, "Statement on Abortion," 1972.
2. The most comprehensive treatment of the subject in English is David M. Feldman, *Marital Relations, Birth Control, and Abortion in Jewish Law* (New York: Schocken, 1974). See also J. David Bleich, "Abortion in Halakhic Literature," and Fred Rosner, "The Jewish Attitude toward Abortion," *Tradition* 10 (Winter 1968).
3. One exception to this is the decision by Rabbi Saul Yisraeli, who ruled that in Thalidomide cases abortion is a favor to the potential child as much as a relief for the mother's anguish. From Responsa Amud Hayemini, no. 32 (1966), as quoted in Feldman, *Marital Relations*, p. 292, n. 134.

4. See Feldman, *Marital Relations*, chs. 14–15.

5. Ibid., pp. 284–94.

6. That mitzvot were commanded for people to live by and not to die by. Classically, this biblical phrase has had a limited legal application; still, the principle is a powerful one and, although not explicitly stated, underlies many halakhic decisions.

7. Irving Greenberg, "Cloud of Smoke, Pillar of Fire," in *Auschwitz: Beginning of a New Era?*, ed. Eva Fleischner (New York: Ktav, 1977).

Feminism and Jewish Survival

I

APPROXIMATELY ten years ago Geraldine Kane (not her real name) started out as a receptionist at ABC-TV in New York. She had just been graduated from Boston University, became involved in a consciousness-raising group, and simultaneously took an assertiveness-training course at New York University. Bright, capable, and newly self-assertive, she quickly rose through the ABC ranks. Today she's a public-relations executive at the network, has her own receptionist, and recently put in a request for a second secretary to help her move along faster. There's every reason to believe that Geri Kane will make it big one day. And why not? For she is as capable as anyone moving up the corporate ladder.

Now Geri's mother, my former neighbor, has mixed feelings about all of this. Proud as she is of her daughter's rapid success, she still wants what she calls a little "Yiddish *nachas*" from Geri. Even in an assimilated home, that still means marriage and children. But Geri has decided never to marry; quite simply, she is in love with her work and the love of no man and no child could compete in that steady passion.

Then there are Barry and Susan, each from solid, middle-class Jewish homes. They met while working together on the Columbia *Law Review*. The following June they were married; the wedding ceremony was performed by her uncle, a prominent Conservative rabbi. Now, seven years later, they have one child, age nineteen months, whose birthday they celebrated with their havurah. Most of their friends in the havurah have one child or none. Only one

157

couple has two. Perhaps some day Barry and Susan will have a second child, but certainly not just yet. If pregnancy should occur, they would have no hesitation about abortion. Recently, Susan was hired by the state comptroller's office, and she wants to stay on the job for at least four years. Between the fifty-hour-a-week baby-sitter and a willing grandmother who lives nearby, Susan and Barry manage their high-pressure dual careers quite well. Two children, they feel, would make it infinitely harder to put the whole thing together.

The impact of feminism cuts across all lines; no segment of the community is safe. Even Rivka, the twenty-seven-year-old Hasidic mother of five, is not immune to the new message. She reads *Redbook* magazine while sitting in the waiting room of the Boro Park mikveh. Silently, she determines to have an IUD inserted. She will pay for the gynecologist's bill in cash; that way, her husband won't be privy—and thus a party—to this transgression.

No one can dispute the fact that feminist values have helped women to take their own lives more seriously and assert greater control over their own destinies. True, feminism is not entirely responsible for the falling birth rate; Zero Population Growth was on the upswing long before feminism gained prominence. But feminist values have had a powerful catalyst effect on the population decline in the Jewish community.

What has changed? Simply this: to previous generations of the Jewish people, the role of wife and mother was the optimal, singular, essential role through which a woman fulfilled herself. Barrenness was synonymous with failure. The biblical commandment "to be fruitful and multiply" was defined by the rabbis as a minimum of two children. In other words, a person should not depart this world leaving behind fewer souls than when he or she entered it. Childlessness after ten years of marriage was considered legitimate grounds for divorce. Rabbinic literature and biblical exegesis reinforced what came quite naturally, the expectation that a woman was to have children, many children, in order to create a good Jewish home and family.

Feminism, however, transmits other messages, primary among them that there is now an enormous range of options open to women, that motherhood is not the only role or even the preferred one. Feminism tells us more: that we can live for ourselves and be fulfilled without meeting the acid test of self-sacrifice. Not too long ago, Sophie Portnoy evoked some sympathy; today she is an archaic, discarded model. Self-sacrifice, which one realistically must make for dependent children, is definitely on the wane. Self-interest ("me, for myself, now") is becoming the dominant mode.

For Jews, then, the message is revolutionary. In previous generations, women had a strong sense of being completely fulfilled as wives and as mothers. No one ever told us before that we should expect something more or something else from ourselves. No one ever told us that our potential was equal to that of those who made the decisions and turned the wheels of society. That idea is mindboggling, particularly to "transition women" who grew up in the thirties, forties, and fifties and were generally content to fill the role set for them. As long as women had their main prop, dependent children, they felt needed, useful, constructive. But now, for the first time in our history, society has spread out a complex set of choices before us and each choice lays claim to our finite time and energies.

Nor is the conflict one only of ideology; it is felt at a very practical level by women who are not willing to relinquish the traditional role of mothering. Children do conflict with career, just as they conflict with other personal goals and other human relationships. Children even conflict with the marriage relationship itself. True, they bind a husband and wife together as nothing else in the world can, but they also usurp other opportunities for deepest expression between two adults. I speak here of privacy—not the "close the bedroom door" variety but rather of time to listen to each other. I speak here too of that particular phenomenon that afflicts every marriage, where conversation about the children seems to preempt all other kinds of shared communication. In these instances the rewards are as great or greater and more than compensate for the conflicts, but in a career the time and energy devoted to one will in some ways diminish the other.

Still, there is no going back on the feminist revolution. It is unrealistic to think that we can stem the flow of women into the wider world simply by telling them to give up their careers, stay home, and have babies for the sake of the Jewish people. The new message about equality and the potential of women is essentially a good one, despite the conflicts it generates. It enables women to grow as individuals, it teaches them to be not so universally dependent on the financial support of men, as women have been; and it can bring only benefit to society.

Furthermore, for many women, work is no longer a matter of choice. Whether women in the work force have or have not contributed to the inflationary spiral, as some economists have suggested, is irrelevant to the young woman who must shoulder or share the responsibility to support herself or her family.

Thus, our best hope for an increased Jewish population, it seems, is to help cope with the areas of conflict and tension, to blend the feminist and traditional models. We must find ways to support and encourage women in the choice of multiple roles of career and motherhood.

II

On a practical level, the most obvious solution and the one most often sought by moderate feminists is full-time day-care centers. The Jewish community needs Jewish day-care centers that specifically fit the Jewish needs of parents and children. In addition, Jewish agencies ought to give lobbying support to the general women's movement on this issue, for we can also benefit from their gains in terms of federal funding and standardized requirements.

I do not find day-care centers to be the best solution, however. I know that as yet there is little scientific data on the positive or negative psychological effect of day-care centers on young children or even on its ultimate impact on population trends. In fact, some researchers have suggested that day-care centers are correlated more accurately with population decline. Beyond that, however, it seems to me that no matter how benign the setting may be, leaving one's young children with surrogate parents for most of their waking hours leaves something to be desired, for both parents and children. I prefer to see other kinds of solutions.

Part-time jobs are an important answer. Here leaders of the

feminist movement subtly have communicated their antifamily bias, for while there have been great efforts to achieve equal pay for equal work for full-time jobs, there have been no similar efforts made for part-time jobs. The overwhelming majority of part-time jobs are staffed by mothers and are notoriously underpaid. Usually, a part-time job means two-thirds of full-time work and one-third of full-time pay. My sister worked for years as director of the social-service department of a New York hospital. She worked from nine to three, four days a week, and was home by four o'clock every day when her three children returned from their Hebrew day schools. She did a good deal of paper and telephone work evenings at home. In other words, she performed a full-time job. The only problem was that she got paid for part-time work. Thus the Jewish community, and particularly the Jewish agencies involved in employment policies, should press for decent pay for part-time jobs everywhere.

In the hiring practice itself, Jewish institutions should serve as models. Each organization should consider where it can restructure certain jobs to fit the part-time needs of mothers. If, for example, two young mothers filled one job, there would probably be no loss in production; both the agency and the women would serve as significant alternate models to the nine-to-five routine.

I know how very easy it is to slip into the pattern of discrimination against mothers of young children. Two years ago I had occasion to hire a secretary. I found that I wasn't really considering women with young children because, I reasoned, they would have to take time off for school vacations, children's illnesses, and the rest. When I casually described to my husband how the hiring task was proceeding, he said to me with great surprise, "Don't you think it's strange, not to say unfair, that you, of all people, are automatically excluding mothers with young children?"

III

Until now, the Jewish community has done very little in the area of career counseling and career reentry. I think these areas will become increasingly significant however, because one of the main influences of feminism has been to encourage women to think in terms of careers and not simply white- or blue-color jobs.

We need better and more family-oriented career counseling. A young woman should know which careers are suited to part-time energies and which can grow naturally from part to full time as more time becomes available. She should know what sort of careers can or cannot be interrupted for a few years. A friend of mine with a biochemistry degree from the Hebrew University worked for several years until she had her first child. Five children and ten years later she wanted to return to her career but quickly learned that she would have to start all over again because so much new and different data had come to light during those ten years. She now edits the scientific writings of others; she just didn't want to spend three more years learning the ropes again. The right kind of counseling from a Jewish perspective could enable women who are really content with the traditional roles of child raising and volunteer communal work to reject the pressures for an immediate career, to resist the coercive trend against motherhood that is now spreading.

It is amazing how the new ideas very nearly have reversed those of a generation or two ago. When the immigrants were trying to make a go of it in the new country, wives, children, anyone who could thread a needle or lift a box was drafted into the work force. A good indication that the family had finally made it was when the mother could retire to home and children. That was women's liberation in the early 1900s. Now it's true that turning a seam or matching a zipper doesn't have quite the same valence as putting together a corporate merger, but the women's movement has tended to overglamorize the creative moments in the work world and underplay those in family and home.

There are still many women, married and with children, who find themselves in the position of not absolutely needing to work for that second income for the family. Sometimes working costs them money, with baby-sitters, transportation, a new tax bracket, and so forth. Still, they feel an intense pressure, almost a guilt, at doing what they are happy doing. For these women, and for society in general, there must be some kind of reminder that not every woman needs to have a job every moment of her adult life in order to feel self-validated. Jewishly oriented career counselors ought to be sensitive to this dimension when talking to women.

If the Jewish agencies are genuine in their concern for population decline, they should establish affirmative-action quotas for mothers, especially for those who want to return to their careers after an extended stint of mothering. Right now, a woman over forty whose children are fairly independent finds it difficult to work her way back into the professional milieu. Similarly, a woman over forty who wants to go back to school to complete her training will find that many of the scholarships and fellowships restrict candidates to those under thirty-five. The logic has always been that if a scholar didn't produce by the age of thirty-five or forty, he would never do so; now, however, the educational trend calls for a different assessment. Such restrictions ought to be labeled for what they are—discrimination against reentering women.

Finally, there ought to be career counseling for couples. In the crunch, why is it the woman who must put her career on the back burner? There are many individual couples who would do best if the husband were to assume the major nurturing role for a few years and allow the wife to pursue her career full time.

I am still sufficiently influenced by history, tradition, anthropology, and biology to perceive of the whole matter in terms of primary and secondary liens on certain roles, with the choice of child-care endeavor falling first to women. I would not like to see it up for grabs in every single relationship. If only from a practical point of view, it could add a strain to many a marriage to have to negotiate from scratch who is primary breadwinner and who is primary nurturer. But the beauty of feminism is that we have learned that one can cross over the lines and blur them, not only sharing but even exchanging roles, without being considered freaks, as would have been the case a generation ago.

The Jewish community faces a particular new problem. Largely as a result of the conflict between career and the open-ended claims of parenthood, we are witnessing a striking rise in the number of women who have a first child in their thirties; by and large, this group tends to have only one child. A startling statistic emerges: by delaying childbirth from the twenties to the thirties, we lose an entire generation every three decades. Career counseling with the Jewish people's needs in mind may temper feminist claims with Jewish ones; it could enable couples to take more seriously the option of having children first and then moving on to dual careers.

In all of these areas of career counseling, Jewish communal agencies cannot afford to wait until the customers show up. They must take the initiative and go to where the people are, in the synagogues, in the centers, and in the educational and social groups.

In this regard there is an urgent need for research. We ought to study more carefully the model of those women who have combined successfully both career and parenting to find out how they cope. Some years ago a study was made of thirty career women in the Orthodox community. These women generally showed a high level of success in managing career, good-sized families, and Jewish obligations. One finding struck me with special force, however. It turns out that the one area that all the women had to sacrifice was their social life. For the last few years, I had been feeling this enormous guilt as I reviewed in my mind the friends I hadn't called, the dinner parties I didn't give, the letters I hadn't written, the overdue gifts. Somehow, finding that this was a perfectly logical, legitimate area to skimp on in light of family and career needs made me feel much less guilty.

I suspect that research on these model women will confirm what personal observations suggest—that traditional Jewish feminists and career women (the two are not synonymous) have more children than nontraditional ones. Whatever the magic ingredient is, we ought to try to spread it around. In other words, it behooves the Jewish federations, educational institutions, and womens' organizations to try to examine how they can communicate more particularist Jewish values and greater observance of the tradition. (This generally has been thought to be the business of the synagogue. But since that is, unfortunately, not where the majority of Jews are these days, other institutions must take up the slack.)

IV

One of the strongest factors in the decision to have fewer children is an economic one. As my brother-in-law put it, "The most effective form of birth control in the Orthodox community today is the day-school tuition rate." Although we don't have a correlation coefficient between birth-control practices and day-school tuition, his statement reflects the reality. I know several young couples in my community who would have had a third or a fourth child were they not burdened with $5,000 to $10,000 a year annual tuition costs.

Federations, therefore, should give more support to day schools and should support and lobby for some means of federal aid to parochial-school education. Until such time as this happens, however, day-school tuitions should be the responsibility of the entire Jewish community and not simply fall on the shoulders of the young couples who have many additional financial burdens at that time in their lives.

Another financial aid is communal support for home child-care services. As it stands right now, a woman who wants to work or go to school and who is not willing to leave her child to the ministrations of a day-care center must either have a husband who can take over or a parent able, willing, and close. Otherwise, she must be very rich, for household help is very dear and part-time jobs barely cover the cost of child care. Many women without these options must wait until the child is in grade school to return to a career. Such a woman often reconsiders her original intention to have more than one or two children because she fears she will be locked in. In such cases Jewish communal subsidy for child care would be invaluable.

Better yet, there is a growing body of the Jewish aged who are capable and willing to work where they will be needed. Older men and women often can serve beautifully in tasks of child care with great patience, and they would feel useful for it as well. Again, Jewish communal agencies should be clearinghouses for distribution of such labor resources.

To be sure, one cringes at the thought of yet another organization in our highly organized community. But if we take population issues seriously there ought to be a central agency that will devote its energies exclusively to this problem. In Israel such an organization was established in 1972, called Zekhuyot Ha-mishpahot Berukhot Yeladim (Zahavi), which translates literally as "rights of families blessed with children." It offers such services as food co-ops and presses for legislation to benefit large families. An organization that will track and coordinate all the support systems—career and personal counseling, child-care services, political pressure activities, family recognition programs, and financial subsidies—would be of great value in this country.

It goes without saying that feminism has had a powerful impact on the rising divorce rate in the Jewish community. An exceedingly high percentage of women involved in feminist organizations are either divorced or single. Divorce takes its toll on population growth because several good childbearing years often are lost until each partner begins to put together the pieces of his or her life. Marriage counseling, to help young Jewish couples integrate the new and unsettling notions of feminism, may do more to increase Jewish population growth than any other single factor.

V

One final issue. There is a group of several thousand persons in our community who desire to have children, who are physically able, but who do not dare for fear of sanction. These are young women in their thirties, mostly well educated, financially independent, and Jewishly committed. They are unmarried, and their prospects of finding a suitable mate shrink from year to year. They are not willing to settle for less than the best just for the sake of getting married.

I have encountered these women in every major city in the United States. On several occasions, after I have finished a lecture on the Jewish family, an attractive, articulate young woman will come up and gently chide me as follows: "You only talk about the family, but what about me? More than anything I want to marry and have children and raise them Jewishly, but I just haven't been able to find the right person to marry. I could manage to raise a child by myself as well as any other single parent. I can't adopt one because the supply is limited and first preference goes to couples. What am I to do?"

I feel some reluctance to raise this issue because I am centered in that community where traditional mores and halakhic boundaries clearly define the Jewish family and such a notion is therefore unsettling. I know too that it is not easy to raise a child with two parents sharing the task, much less so with one parent. Still, those who have known the incredible sweetness of raising children cannot but be sensitive to the needs of these women. At the very least, the community ought to acknowledge the problem and thrash it through.

The implications for social policy are enormous and complex. The halakhic issues must be analyzed; the medical, ethical, and social issues articulated. Questions concerning artificial insemination, genetic counseling, synagogue, and school attitudes toward the children of single women are all part of the broader issue. Perhaps we will have to respond with halakhic categories such as *le-hathila* and *be-di-eved*, differential responses before and after the fact. Perhaps the most positive effect of such discussions will be to jog the communal leaders and agencies into more intensified matchmaking efforts on behalf of such singles.

VI

Beyond all the practical solutions suggested above, there must be support for Jewish population growth at the level of ideas and experiences. I call this support system "the case for Jewish children." The case can be made from many perspectives—halakhic, psychological, ecological (recycling of the nuturing process), the pleasure principle (otherwise known as *nachas*), to name a few.

Each woman, in order to succeed, must arrive at her own unique solution. What works for one won't work for another. Some careers can be handled from the home, some not. Some women simply have a need to get away from the house for a while. The community, however, must generate support systems that help a woman find her own way. That is why the ideological support system is so important. If a woman and man are provided with the right orientation, they somehow will find a way to create a family, no matter what their personal circumstances might be.

The case for Jewish children also can be made from another perspective, a feminist one. This takes form both as a critique of a narrow, coercive interpretation of feminist values and as a broader explication of what a real feminist understanding should be. True feminism means that a woman is free to make the most of her life and herself. If one thinks of self-actualization in its most limited sense, then a career is the answer and all women are squeezed into this new circumscribed role, just as they once were confined to the singular role of wife and mother. As Jews, we must articulate a wider definition, one that includes the following: the experience of extending the biologically natural role to one in which the soul, the character, the sensations are all stretched to their outer limits; a role in which the intense encounter, the ability to give and receive love, and the act of giving of one's self must be perceived as a significant expression of the feminine self. Child raising must be understood from the perspective of a woman's total life, not competing and colliding with other options but complementing them as one phase of a woman's life, optimally exercised within a given biological time, which is a central challenge in the total process of fulfilling one's potential.

VII

Each of us makes personal choices in life; then we proceed to rationalize our choice as part of some legitimate world view. Mine, I think, can be articulated best as a positive theory of conflict. For I find myself squarely located among those women whose primary orientation is as a traditional Jew, with all the family values and obligations that entails, but who are at the same time attracted to feminist notions of equality, expanding horizons, self-growth.

So I live with the conflict. I live with it every day, in a thousand ways that pull me in one direction or another. I have come to realize that the conflict is a sign of my health, not of my confusion; the tension is a measure of the richness of my life, not of its disorderliness. It is a sign that I am trying to have the best of both worlds—the traditional richness of the Jewish family and the new chances for personal growth that feminism offers me in ways that society never offered my mother or grandmothers.

When I stop feeling the conflict, I will know that one phase of my life is over. At that point, I hope I will look back without regrets that I missed something precious. I hope I will look back with a great sense of pleasure that I was fortunate enough to have taken the fullest advantage of the very special gifts given to me and to have done so at just the perfect moment in my life.

Afterword: Some Loose Ends

I

IT has been suggested that Jewish feminists are not all they pur-
port to be, that they are guilty of wanting the best of all worlds
at no cost, that they are up to nothing more than a futile or silly
attempt to make traditional Judaism chic. This accusation is most
odd, for not only does it misrepresent Jewish feminism, but deep
down it also betrays a frightened and frightening siege mentality,
a way of thinking about tradition and ritual that is unbecoming
and that does either little justice. Jewish feminists have no interest
in making Orthodoxy fashionable, or modern, or relevant, or anything else.

It never will be chic to observe a real Shabbat as long as society
glorifies the unrestrained, unrestricted life style of "Saturday's
generation." Nor to spend precious hours studying Torah and
Talmud, which won't qualify you for a high-paying job or provide
scintillating dinner-party conversation. Nor to pray daily in an age
that sets store by self-made, self-centered men and women. Nor to
observe kashrut when one set of dishes and a multi-ethnic cuisine
will do. Nor to abstain from sex twelve days a month, followed by
a visit to the mikveh, when sex as the mood strikes you is the
unquestioned norm. Nor to observe marital fidelity when affairs
are now a sign of liberation of the sexes. Nor to raise a Jewish
family when the times direct you to "go your own way." Nor to
give a tithe of one's income to charity and another tenth for
yeshiva education for one's children when upwardly mobile families could use the money elsewhere.

No, I do not wish to make Orthodoxy chic, for I believe—as I have experienced it—that a life lived according to Halakhah is a most worthwhile life, a richly textured life, in fact, a blessed life.

But, yes, I do want the best of both worlds, that is, using the best insights of each to enrich the other. And despite the difficulties of reconciling the tension between the two, why should I not want the best of both, for I am a committed Jew and I am also a woman. I want to live my life as a halakhic Jew, but I do not believe for a single moment that the divine plan for this world was to have women eternally consigned to second-class status, or none at all, in significant areas of our religious and cultural life. Nor do I believe that the system will crumble and shred if women are given first-class status. I do not want to reject the basics. All I ask is that women have equal access to them.

II

This brings me to the second point, a question that begets a hundred others, a question we must ask though we fumble for answers. If men and women have equal access and equal responsibility, how can we define male and female beyond pure biology? In what ways can we communicate to the next generation a healthy sense of sexual identity?

These questions rest on the premise that there is a cosmic need to draw some lines, a larger purpose—including preservation of the species, but also going beyond it—in strengthening sexual identity. To put it another way, if the lines are blurred in everything but anatomy, if male and female become interchangeable concepts, then perhaps what awaits us down the road is not perfect equality but pure confusion.

Now all of this makes some feminists very uncomfortable, even hostile. For they assume that sex differences necessarily imply a hierarchy, and hierarchies mean differential rewards, an uneven dividing of the pie. Besides, these are issues that divide. There are a good number of trade-offs one must make for full equality, and many are not willing to make them.

Nevertheless, the questions remain, punching holes in an ideal vision. There are signals that we cannot overlook as we begin to search for outlines. Equality clearly does not mean sameness. Nor is physiological function the whole difference. Social scientists now inform us that there are many differences in male and female behavior that in no way are the result of different socialization of the sexes. Running parallel with the new equality, and perhaps growing out of it, is an emerging body of literature that probes and defines the essence of male and female, not in terms of physical characteristics but rather behavioral ones. The definitions seem to be finer, more detailed, and slightly different from the ones we inherited.

New research also confirms what we see all around us—the remarkable staying power of classic men's and women's roles in society. One may lightly pass this off as the result of centuries of conditioning. But whole societies do not grow in embryo; they are shaped in the ground of human history. Powerful as the new ideology is, anthropological memories are much more pervasive. One must account for memories even as one dreams of restructuring society.

An odd thing happened to me several years ago regarding "female" tasks. In 1974, my eighteen-year-old nephew Natan was serving in the Israeli army. (He had made aliyah on his own a year earlier, just before the Yom Kippur War.) During our sabbatical in Jerusalem that year we became his surrogate family. This meant that every third or fourth week he would come home to us on weekend furlough.

Like most family-oriented transition women, I have done a good amount of cooking and cleaning in the last two decades. Like most, I approached these chores as chores. Sometimes they were an escape, a chance to let the mind wander, daydream. Mostly, however, I was acutely aware that the drudgery was getting in the way of something more meaningful, like human relationships or career. Many times, as I folded endless piles of clothing, I thought: What is a woman with my years of schooling doing wasting her life on mindless laundry! Whenever possible I would push these tasks off on someone else, hired or drafted. At no time did I get the thrill the TV commercials promised. I did the job simply because it had to get done.

Now, strangely, I found myself waiting to cook for our young soldier, to feed him, to do his laundry. There was a powerful primal emotion associated with these mundane tasks, almost a sacredness about them. I felt a certain pleasure in knowing that I had a repeated part in repairing that spent and dusty frame.

I began to wonder. Was it simply my share of the national effort? Was it an impulse akin to caring for a sick child? Or was it a feeling that grew out of some archetypal feminine source, as much a part of me as my womb? Whatever, it was a feeling, I since have learned, that it is universally shared by Israeli women for their soldier sons, husbands, and brothers. This is not to say that Israeli women lay all their other work aside, or that men are any less caring and concerned. It is to say that there are perhaps differential responses that can be characterized as male and female. One should not get caught in a trap of labeling as sexist every differential response until one has examined whether it falls on the side of distinctiveness or discrimination.

From other sectors of society we know that a solution of separate but equal tends to fail. Unlike other groups, however, men and women will always need each other. Separatist solutions will be sought only by the radical fringes of the women's movement. Perhaps a theme of distinctive but equal is more healthy, more realistic, more flexible than notions of absolute equality, which inevitably will break down in a web of uniform expectations.

Distinctive but equal may also help to resolve the sticky issue of trade-offs. Here there are many questions. What kind of trade-offs must we make, men and women alike, for real equality? How necessary are certain trade-offs? How consistent must we be?

If, as I have maintained, the distinctions between male and female in biblical and rabbinic times were pragmatic and not rigid, the distinctive-but-equal model can apply to Judaism as well. Now, women may—ought—to have access to the larger areas: the study of Torah, prayer, the power of making decisions, rabbinic leadership. Within these broadly encompassing areas there can be fine distinctions between male and female regarding specific smaller rituals associated with each sex—not a "his and her" religion but one that manages to allow for distinctiveness of the sexes as it engenders an expansive sense of equality. This will mean lifting an entire set of taboos for women. A model to follow is that of

Sabbath candlelighting. This is a mitzvah that falls to women, yet any man may do it. There is no hands-off policy, as there is for women performing men's mitzvot.

I have the feeling that what ultimately will emerge from all the unsettling effect feminism has had upon Jews committed to tradition is a more delicate drawing of the lines. And it will happen quietly, in bits and pieces, until such time as it is legislated from on high.

A final illustration. Recently, a newlywed couple spent a Shabbat with us in Jerusalem. He is a yeshiva student, four long tzitzit hanging out for all the world to see; she covers her hair. For all that, they are open in their thinking, modern in their ways, exemplars of the new, modern Orthodoxy. On Friday night I placed a kiddush cup and two hallahs at his table setting. Without calling any attention to himself, he transferred the loaves to his wife's setting. I thought it was simply to give himself room, but after the ritual hand washing she recited the blessing over the bread—softly, but all alone. On Shabbat day the same thing happened. It then became perfectly clear that they had discussed the issue, had checked the halakhic sources, and had decided how properly to share the two Sabbath responsibilities, as well as the head of household roles each symbolizes.

III

Not every change will be made as gracefully as that of a young romantic couple looking for ways to share each other's lives more fully. Undoubtedly there will be much haggling, bickering, protest, insult, fear, anxiety, rationalization, and sublimation until a position of equality in Judaism stabilizes. One hopes that women and men will understand this in its proper perspective, as a process on the way toward a goal.

Like any other successful revolution, and like the broader women's movement, Jewish feminism ought to look toward the day when it can self-destruct. Until that moment, and long after it, we ought to keep our eye on the main target. That, I believe, is the real message of the women's movement, a message in universal language that we as Jews must particularize. The message is an old one, as old as the prophets themselves. Perhaps it is being spoken to women for the first time in our lives—that now we too are responsible for the whole of society.

As a transition woman, I always have found it natural to say, "Someone else should do it." I have sat back and criticized this or that aspect of society. Why, I've been asking myself for years, isn't there stricter gun control? Why is there recoil from the poor? Why are rapists returned to the streets? Why isn't there more cancer research? Why this, why not that? Why don't *they* do something about it?

Suddenly it occurred to me that part of my liberation as a woman is that I also am responsible for what goes on in the world. If this society fails, it is also my failure. I must give up that old fantasy, that habit of watching and waiting. If something is doable, then women must get on with the task. They must bring their fresh talents and idealism to improve and upgrade society.

So too with Jewish feminism. We must leap from the universal to the particular. We are responsible for Jewish problems, for the future of the community, for the continuity of tradition, for Israel, for Jews everywhere.

IV

I have now had my say, but my thinking on the matters I have discussed in this book is unfinished. In fact, in many ways I am still at a midpoint in coming to an understanding of what impact feminism ultimately will have on Judaism and on human relationships as defined by Judaism. For one thing, there is such limited information at this point that it is simply too soon to arrive at any firm conclusion with any great feelings of confidence. Second, my thinking is unfinished because my own emotions, as well as the emotions and perceptions of many people at all points of the spectrum—people who matter a great deal to me—often clash headlong with each other and with the raw logical formulations. Although I have learned much in the course of setting my ideas down on paper, even more than that, I have become aware of how much there is yet to understand about the subject—the intricate and vast sources, the internal dynamic, the interrelationships of society, law, emotions, habit, conditioning, sexuality, and faith.

I have been engaged in a great deal of gentle arguing during the last few years, much of it with myself. Each time I seemed to nail down an idea, something would happen to make it come apart. Inevitably, I would have to begin to sort it out all over again. Just when I thought I had the most sensible Jewish response to abortion where Tay-Sachs fetuses are concerned, I'd meet a woman who would tell me: "Even knowing what I know now, the agony we went through for four years [until the Tay-Sachs child died], I still don't think I would want an abortion. There was so much love there." Just when I propounded the thesis that having a Jewish child is the most creative and deeply religious act a woman can do, a slip of a woman tells me that she will never marry and never have children but will devote her life to Jewish education, just as her renowned teacher did. For all my confident responses, I would find myself hours later consumed with doubt, trying to climb out of a pit of confusion over the genuine problem that has *not yet* been addressed by feminism: how, in fact, can we transmit messages about sexual identity if not through distinct functions? Just when I concluded that it borders on obscenity not to count a women as part of a *mezuman* (the quorum for grace after meals)— a woman who has organized, prepared, and served a meal to her family—I would find my own teenage sons, who are (mostly) models of filial love and respect, vehemently disagree.

All this makes me quite vulnerable. In fact, I find it hard to resist writing my own critique of the work. It's an easy enough task, given the inconsistencies: calling for equality and freedom of choice, yet maintaining that there are primary and secondary models of behavior for men and women; calling for specific mitzvot for male and female without satisfactorily fleshing them out; calling for a love for Halakhah and tradition, yet subtly tearing away at parts of its intricate tapestry, perhaps weakening other threads in the process. And yet . . .

Perhaps this is the only legitimate response one can make at this time: a series of tentative remarks. If feminism is a revolution, as I believe it is, and Judaism is and always has been the rock-bottom source of a Jew's values, thoughts, feelings, actions, mores, laws, and loves—how else can one respond to and be part of that turbulent encounter but with a stammer, one step forward and half a step backward. I envy those who can say, "This is Halakhah. That's it!" Or, "These are the absolute new truths, and nothing less will do!" I envy, but I also suspect, their unexamined complacency. I suspect that their fear is even greater than mine; therefore, they must keep the lid on even tighter and show no ambivalence, no caution, and no confusion.

So for me, despite the turbulence, or maybe because of it, it has not been all bad. I have had some very good feelings in the course of doing this work. The best of these has been a sense of being able to approach the sources without intimidation. The fact that I can think about the traditional sources without knowing them exhaustively, that I can bring to bear my own interpretative keys without diminishing the divinity and authority of the Halakhah and tradition—this has been a revelation for me. So, too, the experience, which all women alive today share, of stretching ourselves, our minds, our talents, our sights. Transition women, like myself, are taking everything less for granted and finding each step more exhilarating.